KILLING CONTENTION

Modern Intellectual and Political History of the Middle East
Fred H. Lawson, *Series Editor*

Select Titles in Modern Intellectual and Political History of the Middle East

The Autocratic Parliament: Power and Legitimacy in Egypt, 1866–2011
Irene Weipert-Fenner

Figures That Speak: The Vocabulary of Turkish Nationalism
Matthew deTar

Hakibbutz Ha'artzi, Mapam, and the Demise of the Israeli Labor Movement
Tal Elmaliach; Haim Watzman, trans.

Iran's Experiment with Parliamentary Governance: The Second Majles, 1909–1911
Mangol Bayat

Islam, Revival, and Reform: Redefining Tradition for the Twenty-First Century
Natana J. DeLong-Bas, ed.

Sayyid Qutb: An Intellectual Biography
Giedrė Šabasevičiūtė

Watermelon Democracy: Egypt's Turbulent Transition
Joshua Stacher

Why Alliances Fail: Islamist and Leftist Coalitions in North Africa
Matt Buehler

For a full list of titles in this series,
visit https://press.syr.edu/supressbook-series
/modern-intellectual-and-political-history-of-the-middle-east/.

KILLING CONTENTION

Demobilization in Morocco during the Arab Spring

SAMMY ZEYAD BADRAN

Syracuse University Press

∞ The paper used in this publication meets the minimum requirements
of the American National Standard for Information Sciences—Permanence
of Paper for Printed Library Materials, ANSI Z39.48-1992.

For a listing of books published and distributed by Syracuse University Press,
visit https://press.syr.edu/.

ISBN: 978-0-8156-3774-5 (hardcover)
978-0-8156-3784-4 (paperback)
978-0-8156-5568-8 (e-book)

Library of Congress Cataloging-in-Publication Data
Names: Badran, Sammy Zeyad, author.
Title: Killing contention : demobilization in Morocco
during the Arab Spring / Sammy Zeyad Badran.
Description: First edition. | Syracuse : Syracuse University Press, 2022. |
Series: Modern intellectual and political history of the Middle East |
Includes bibliographical references and index.
Identifiers: LCCN 2022019237 (print) | LCCN 2022019238 (ebook) |
ISBN 9780815637745 (hardcover) | ISBN 9780815637844 (paperback) |
ISBN 9780815655688 (ebook)
Subjects: LCSH: Morocco—History—Demonstrations, 2011–2012. | February 20
Movement (Morocco) | Protest movements—Morocco. | Political participation—
Morocco. | Morocco—Politics and government—1999–
Classification: LCC DT326.3 .B33 2022 (print) | LCC DT326.3 (ebook) |
DDC 964.05/3—dc23/eng/20220802
LC record available at https://lccn.loc.gov/2022019237
LC ebook record available at https://lccn.loc.gov/2022019238

Manufactured in the United States of America

Contents

Illustrations

Figures

Tables

Acknowledgments

Throughout my time in Morocco, interviewees graciously offered their time and knowledge, and without them, this book would not have been possible. Unfortunately, I am unable to name the individuals I had the honor to meet, but I would like to express my general gratitude to all the youth activists, political organizations, politicians, academics, and journalists who opened their offices and homes to me. The hospitality, kindness, and humility of interviewees, acquaintances, and friends throughout Morocco have been inspiring.

This book would not have been possible without the support from advisers, professors, colleagues, friends, and family. The idea for the book started in 2015 at the University of Kansas. As a graduate student at KU, I was supported by the Department of Political Science. I am indebted to the dedication, support, and patience from my academic advisers, Hannah Britton and Gail Buttorff. As a professor, I now understand all of the time and effort they put into this project. I would like to thank professors, mentors, and committee members at KU, including Gary Reich, Nazli Avdan, Don Haider-Markel, Micheal Wuthrich, and Alesha Doan. Thank you all for your advice and support. I also thank all of my Arabic instructors, both at KU and in Morocco, who provided me with the tools to conduct interviews in Morocco. I am also indebted to the kind professors at the University of Hawaii at Manoa, Political Science Department, where my interest in contentious politics and critical political outlook began— thank you: Jairus Grove, Michael J. Shapiro, Noelani Goodyear-Ka'ōpua, and Sankaran Krishna.

Since starting this project, I have been fortunate to cross paths with many remarkable acquaintances, colleagues, and amazing scholars at conferences, during fieldwork, and at various institutions, including Brian Turnbull, Ginger Feather, Ranya Ahmed, Fassue Kelleh, Marcy Quiason, Luke Herrington, Cagil Albayrak, Corolina Candal, Laura Dean, Jacob Longaker, Brittnee Carter, Ryan Daugherty, Caroline Abadeer, Mehran Kamrava, Graham Cornwell, Chouki el Hamel, Jeneice Lusk, Jeff King, Bethany Shockley, Isa Blumi, Giacomo Chiozza, Matteo Salvadore, Johannes Van Gorp, Kristina Katsos, Vernon Pedersen, and Yuting Wang. I would like to especially thank Matt Buehler, who was kind enough to offer me valuable advice about Moroccan politics since I began my book project. A special thanks to Brian Turnbull, a friend and colleague who has been supportive since we met in grad school.

I am most grateful to my life partner, Mar, and my son, Noor. I could not have finished this project without Mar's unconditional love and continuous support and without Noor's much-needed distractions from work. I can't fathom being able to complete this project without both of you—*los amo*. I am forever grateful to my parents, Rola and Zeyad, for their lifelong love and support—my interest in politics was instilled at an early age by loud discussions with both my parents—and thank you for everything, Mama and Baba. I appreciate love and support from my family and friends, especially Rosmary, Greg, Reda, Saida, Jason, Paulina, Nader, Haney, and Frank.

As is the case with most research, funding was critical for this project. I am very thankful for the Fulbright Program, which allowed me to travel to Morocco for nine months of fieldwork. I am also grateful for the Moroccan-American Commission for Educational & Cultural Exchange and James Miller for their support. Financial support was also provided by the University of Kansas Sociology Department and the Kansas African Studies Center, which generously funded my language training through the Foreign Language and Area Studies Fellowship. Previous manuscripts and articles in the book received indispensable feedback at conferences and papers. I appreciate the valuable feedback received at the 2019 Southern Political Science Association Conference, 2018 American Political Science Association Conference, 2018 Arab Graduate Student Conference in Doha, and the Twenty-Fourth Annual Moroccan Studies Symposium in Rabat.

Finally, I am indebted to the peer reviewers recruited by Syracuse University Press for their thorough, thoughtful, and invaluable feedback. I thank the book's series editor, Fred H. Lawson, and the acquisitions editor, Peggy Solic, for their kind assistance and suggestions as well.

Parts of the book are derived from past publications, including my article published in the *Journal of North African Studies*: "Demobilising the February 20 Movement in Morocco: Regime Strategies during the Arab Spring," https://www.tandfonline.com/doi/abs/10.1080/13629387.2019.16 34558, https://doi.org/10.1080/13629387.2019.1634558. Table 2 is from this article and reprinted with permission. Chapter 4 is derived, in part, from my article "Signaling Reforms through Election Results: How a Moroccan Opposition Party Demobilized Protests," *British Journal of Middle Eastern Studies* (copyright © 2019 British Society of Middle Eastern Studies), reprinted by permission of Informa UK Limited, trading as Taylor & Francis Group, www.tandfonline.com, on behalf of British Society of Middle Eastern Studies, https://doi.org/10.1080/13530194.2019.1651634). Table 4 is from this article and reprinted with permission.

Abbreviations

AMDH	Moroccan Association for Human Rights
CDT	Democratic Confederation of Labor
DWP	Democratic Way Party
F20	February 20 Movement
JCO	Justice and Charity Organization
MALI	Alternative Movement for Personal Liberties
MP	Popular Movement
MPDC	Popular Democratic and Constitutional Movement
PAM	Authenticity and Modernity Party
PJD	Party of Justice and Development
UC	Constitutional Union
UGTT	Tunisian General Labor Union
UMT	Moroccan Workers Union
USFP	Socialist Union of Popular Forces
USP	United Socialist Party

KILLING CONTENTION

Introduction

Abdul was beaten and harassed, and he spent time in prison for his involvement in illegal protests. Considering what he had been through, I did not expect him to agree to an interview concerning his activism.[1] Following a brief conversation on the phone, Abdul agreed to meet me in exactly four hours at a location he would reveal a few minutes before the meeting. An hour later Abdul told me to meet him at the Rabat Ville Train Station—a centrally located and bustling part of the Moroccan capital. He punctually arrived wearing a Palestinian kaffiyeh around his neck and a skin-tight gray sweater. Abdul said we would have the interview at a nearby bar where his friends were waiting for him. Abdul seemed ready to end the interview, which mostly focused on his ordeals with the police and why the leftist-Islamist alliance within the movement withered. Before leaving, however, he ended the conversation on a surprisingly hopeful note. He indicated that although the February 20 Movement (F20) was no longer active, there was hope that democratic changes would occur in his country. "Islamists do not practice democracy, they use it as a tool to reach power," Abdul insisted, "but there is still hope: the upcoming elections." To my surprise, Abdul knew that Islamists would likely win the second parliamentary elections since the 2011 Middle East and North Africa (MENA) Uprisings (they did), but he was still planning on casting his ballot. He no longer believed in fighting for change through the social movement he helped create. Despite the common sentiment among fellow socialist allies that the elections were only for Islamists to take

---

1. I use pseudonyms for all interviewees rather than real names.

advantage of, Abdul stressed that "the only way for us to change our social and political situation is by voting." I was perplexed by how a militant-Marxist activist and outspoken critic of the Makhzen—a commonly used Moroccan term to denote the traditional system of power and political authority—was now apparently convinced that change through elections, that Islamists were projected to win, was the "only way" forward. I quickly realized that members of the movement had vastly different opinions concerning how democratic change could occur in the country. Indeed, most interviewees expressed their disappointment in the king's concessions and vowed that increasing pressure through street protests was the only path forward. Abdul, however, accepted that the movement accomplished its main goals. I asked Abdul about the future of the movement, to which he responded that "no social movement lives forever," but a movement would form again when needed, depending on the "circumstances, demands, and political conditions."

Roughly two months after my interview with Abdul, Mouchine Fikri, a thirty-one-year-old fishmonger from Al-Hoceima, had five hundred kilograms of swordfish seized and disposed of by local authorities because it was illegally fished out of season on October 28, 2016. Fikri was forced into the shadow economy owing to a lack of opportunities, unemployment, and poverty—especially common in Al-Hoceima and the Moroccan Rif.[2] He was crushed to death inside a garbage truck while trying to salvage his fish. According to witnesses, authorities told the truck driver to "crush him," and the driver pushed the button that killed Fikri.[3] The next day, Fikri's disfigured face was on the front page of most Moroccan newspapers. The Hirak-al-Rif movement was born.

Interviewees tended to view the Hirak-al-Rif as a continuation of the F20. Indeed, many F20 cofounders and activists were organizers in

2. According to a World Bank study, nearly 38 percent of the Moroccan labor force is informal, which is common in the region among resource-poor/labor-rich economies (Gatti et al. 2014).

3. "It Could Happen to Any of Us: Why the Revolution in Morocco Has Started," *Middle East Eye*, Nov. 1, 2016, https://www.middleeasteye.net/opinion/it-could-happen-any-us-why-revolution-morocco-has-started.

the Hirak-al-Rif movement. However, unlike the F20, the Hirak-al-Rif is rooted in the Rif region's marginalization. Nevertheless, the Hirak-al-Rif eventually led to national protests, and many of the activists I interviewed were now, again, taking to the streets.

The 2011 MENA Uprisings

The outrage following Fikri's death echoed what occurred six years prior when protests erupted in Tunisia on December 18, 2010, one day after the self-immolation of Mohamed Bouazizi, a Tunisian street vendor who was mistreated by local police. The demonstrations continued for twenty-eight days until Tunisian president Zine El Abidine Ben Ali fled the country. Inspired by the events in Tunisia, Egyptians took to the streets on January 25, 2011, and violent and nonviolent demonstrations engulfed the nation until President Hosni Mubarak was forced from power. By February 2012, the leaders of Libya and Yemen were ousted following mass protests, while protests and major uprisings spread throughout Algeria, Morocco, Iraq, Kuwait, Bahrain, Jordan, and Sudan.

The uprisings engulfed some countries within the region, but many remained relatively unaffected. Some governments at the forefront of the uprisings, like those of Egypt and Tunisia, reacted overwhelmingly with repressive measures against protesters. Morocco responded differently by offering and implementing constitutional reforms in response to protests. Indeed, some have suggested that the Moroccan king learned that harsh repression could backfire after the ouster of both the Egyptian and the Tunisian presidents (Hamblin 2015). Nevertheless, the fact that protests ensued well after reforms were declared in Morocco casts doubt on explanations that link top-down reforms to the abatement of protests in Morocco and elsewhere in the MENA.

Like citizens of other countries of the region, Moroccans were inspired by the events in Tunisia and Egypt. Nine days after the ouster of Hosni Mubarak in Egypt, thousands of Moroccans began protesting in the capital of Rabat on February 20, 2011. However, unlike other countries, Moroccans did not initially call for the ouster of the king and did not use the slogan heard in other Middle East and North African countries: "The people want to bring down the regime." Rather, Moroccan protesters initially demanded reforms to the constitution, specifically a transition from an executive monarchy to a democratic parliamentary monarchy.

In explaining the 2011 uprisings in Morocco, current scholarly approaches tend to overlook the protest movements themselves when attempting to explain both why protests abated in Morocco and why protests did not engulf and destabilize the country (Benchemsi 2014; Desrues 2013; Lawrence 2017). How these internal social movement dynamics interact with state policies offers insights into the underresearched topic of why protests abate. I argue that the announcement of constitutional reforms by King Mohammed VI on March 9, 2011, did not independently demobilize the February 20 Movement.

The Central Argument

This book aims to understand why protests abate by investigating how and why social movements demobilize. In other words, I investigate why and how activists, like Abdul, abandon street protests. I do so by questioning the causal link between consistent policies (concessions or repression) and social movement demobilization. The term *demobilization* has been used by various social movement theorists, each with differing definitions (Edwards and Marullo 1995; Humphreys and Weinstein 2007; Davenport 2015). I partially adopt Davenport's definition and label demobilization as the "termination of or significant reduction in dissident interventions" and the "departure of individuals (members) from relevant organizations" (2015, 21). I label demobilization as the departure of organizational support from a social movement, while I use the term *protest decline* to refer to the general abatement/ceasing of protest activity.

To understand demobilization, I develop a framework to better understand how internal social movement dynamics along with regime strategies led to successful, and relatively peaceful, demobilization. More specifically, my theory shows how a calculated mix of accommodation followed by repression successfully demobilized a social movement.

The book will outline how the Moroccan regime's policy of announcing concessions followed by repression demobilized the F20. As we will see, this "mixed policy" demobilized the F20 owing to three important factors. First, the Moroccan king has a history of not just declaring but implementing proposed reforms. In the next chapter, I outline how King Mohammed VI has usually implemented reforms in response to grievances from civil society. Second, keeping in mind the reformist nature of the regime, implementing concessions signaled to activists and the Moroccan public that the F20's grievances were addressed. This implementation essentially convinced some F20 activists to leave the streets, with many deciding to cast ballots during the 2011 national election. Third, repression used against the F20 led to a divergence between the F20 and the general public, which overwhelmingly supports the king and feared that Morocco may transgress into violence, as was occurring at the time in Libya and Syria. This departure demobilized the F20 and alienated it from society. The book will outline how the F20's more revolutionary elements not only internally divided the movement, but also convinced reformist activists and the public that there was no longer a need for a social movement since unprecedented reforms were being implemented.

The accepted wisdom from the trajectory of the 2011 MENA Uprisings in Morocco is that reforms led to a decline in protests. Sean Yom and Gregory Gause note that the leaders of Morocco along with Jordan "reacted to growing unrest with political-liberalization initiatives that have satisfied some opposition demands and helped to stanch protests" (2012, 79). This observation, however, has not been empirically supported or deeply analyzed. As this book demonstrates, the king's calculated use of various concessions followed by repression convinced Moroccans that change through reforms and state institutions was a sufficient response to the F20's grievances. This book will show how the F20 became a divided movement that could not uniformly respond to a series of concessions followed by repression and how the public became convinced that there was no longer a need for a social movement for change.

In the Field

Social movement scholar Christian Davenport correctly notes that prior research on social movement demobilization tends to ignore the sequencing and timing of demobilization. Specifically, Davenport tells us they ignore that "specific sequences or events that happened earlier might have important influences on what takes place." To better understand the relationship between repression and demobilization, Davenport believes "the best way to study the topic is to systematically evaluate discussions, actions, and relationships between members of social movement organizations" (2015, 10). Although I did not have access to "dissident gatherings," which Davenport did, my interviews did reveal a trove of information about discussions that occurred within F20 committee meetings and political party meetings.

From September 2016 to May 2017, I conducted forty-six semistructured interviews with participants from the F20. Apart from two journalists who participated and reported on the movement, all interviewees were activists within the F20 movement from various political parties and organizations. My main method of gaining interviewees was via the chain-of-referral method, where interviewees identified other potential interviewees. A purposeful sample method was implemented based on organization type, and within each organization I interviewed elites (general secretaries, executive directors, party figureheads, F20 cofounders) and active members. I interviewed a proportional number of people from each main organization (Islamists/leftists/independents) within the F20 until saturation was reached.

The information and range of topics I discussed during my interviews were wide; however, for this book, I examine themes related to the abatement of F20 protests. My discussions included direct and indirect references to F20 protests, ideological conflicts and alliances following concessions and repression, and external regional factors that played a role in the movement's momentum. Interviews were conducted with activists from various cities, including Rabat, Casablanca, Tangier, Agadir, Marrakech, Meknes, Tétouan, M'rirt, and Berkane. Most of my interviews were conducted in Arabic, while some were conducted in English and Spanish. All interviews were transcribed into English. The evidence for my findings relies on my interviews, but I also conducted archival research, primarily relying on the Arabic-language newspaper *Hespress*.

Why Morocco?

Morocco has often been treated as an afterthought within studies specific to the 2011 MENA Uprisings. Some claim that there were only limited protests that did not lead to mass uprisings (that is, Tunisia and Egypt) in Morocco (Brownlee, Masoud, and Reynolds 2015). Many studies do not include Morocco in their analyses of the 2011 MENA Uprisings (Haas and Lesch 2013; Noueihed and Warren 2012; Gelvin 2015; Culbertson 2016; Çakmak 2017). Any researcher who has spent time in Morocco will quickly realize how important the F20 protests of 2011–12 were for Moroccans. Many interviewees express a sense that their country would not have so narrowly avoided following the violent paths of Yemen or Syria had protests not subsided in 2012 (see chapter 5).[4]

It is safe to conclude that "state violence was the political fulcrum of the Arab Spring" (Brownlee, Masoud, and Reynolds 2015, 41).[5] Within Morocco, however, repression did influence the F20, but reforms and concessions were the first tools used by the state. This factor makes Morocco a unique case within the MENA that merits in-depth investigation. Moreover, the unprecedented dynamics of the cross-ideological alliances within Morocco are also unique and merit study since there is an infrequent prehistory of Islamist/leftist coalitions prior to the F20 in Morocco (Wegner and Pellicer 2011). Rather, the Moroccan case demonstrates how organizations that used to violently engage with one another can, in a short period of time, unite under the banner of one social movement, which was unprecedented for Morocco. This unity was not the case in the other MENA monarchy that responded to protests primarily with reforms— Jordan, where liberals, Islamists, and tribal leaders were not united under a single-umbrella social movement (Yitzhak 2017). Furthermore, unlike in Morocco, demands in Jordan focused on improving the economic situation, and reforms were followed by lessening protests, not an increase, as we see in Morocco.

In Morocco, the monarchy realized that historically antagonistic groups united early on, and, therefore, the campaign to demobilize the F20 targeted separate organizations, sometimes with clear success. For

4. Independent activist, interview with the author, Sept. 22, 2016, Mohammedia.
5. The term *2011 MENA Uprisings* will be used in lieu of *Arab Spring* throughout the book.

instance, the king's decision to pardon 146, mostly Islamist-Salafist, prisoners precipitated the end of organized Salafist involvement in the F20. Similarly, the early decision to talk with unions and concede to their demands also removed a large sector of the population from potentially joining the F20.

Therefore, this book analyzes the case of Morocco in order to reveal how a unique case of major reforms followed by repression affects social movements, how allowing (that is, not changing electoral rules or redistricting) previously sidelined Islamists to win general elections works in favor of regime persistence and stability, how environmental changes via concessions and repression affected internal cross-ideological alliances, and how a movement's "horizontal" structure facilitated demobilization.

Road Map

Chapter 1 will situate the book within broader findings within social movement studies. I outline a theory that demonstrates how concessions followed by selective repression demobilize social movements. The theoretical framework explains how this "mixed"-state policy can abate protests. Chapter 1 also engages feminist methodology and how identity may simultaneously open and close doors to activist networks in Morocco.

Chapter 2 demonstrates that changes in the political environment interact with social movement framing processes that may lead to their decline. I use an alternative approach that analyzes how external policies interact with internal factors to demonstrate when demobilization will likely occur. I show that when social movements face a crisis, they focus on maintaining relevance and resonance with the public. In this stage, movements typically experiment with prognostic frames to test resonance with the public and state reactions; however, the F20 was not united in how to best resonate with the public. This lack of unity resulted in a variance of prognostic frames, ranging from reformist to revolutionary. The divide between what activists characterize as reformist monarchists and more revolutionary republicans became more visible following the king's speech on March 9, 2011, and especially leading up to the king's second major announcement concerning the new constitution in June 2011. The

F20's message became inconsistent and less relevant when the king systematically responded to demands with reforms.

Chapter 3 outlines how the civil wars in Libya and Syria served as an opportunity for the regime to convince the general public of the danger that continued street protests would cause. The images of conflict in both contexts made Moroccans especially fearful of sectarianism and the potential rise of violent Islamists to power. The regime's smear campaign successfully framed the F20 as extreme and composed of fringe groups that hoped for radical/revolutionary change. In essence, the F20 became viewed as increasingly incompatible with many Moroccans. Direct repression was strategically used by the king after major concessions were offered, and the F20 was increasingly viewed as extreme. This chapter demonstrates how the timing and aim of repression matter. Repression against protests is typically aimed at immediately dispersing protests. In Morocco, however, the primary goal of repression was to delegitimize and fracture a social movement. Direct repression was thus timed to occur when the movement, in the words of one activist, "exhausted its purpose." Direct repression along with the calculated use of *baltagiya* (government-paid thugs), following the March 9 speech, were aimed at sending signals to a public that was all too aware of the regional uprisings and the potential for instability and violence. This repression campaign led to an increased divide between reformists and revolutionaries regarding the direction the movement should take.

Chapter 4 will demonstrate how the early parliamentary elections of 2011 affected the momentum of the F20. Elections within authoritarian contexts and social movements have been thoroughly, yet separately, studied. This chapter jointly analyzes these different phenomena in order to demonstrate how electoral results can affect protest demobilization. I begin with the premise that "an election is a public signal observed by a group of citizens before they decide whether to take anti-regime action" (Little, Tucker, and LaGatta 2015, 1144). This chapter argues that a parliamentary victory of a sidelined Islamist party, the Party of Justice and Development (PJD), which had not previously held parliamentary plurality, played a major role in ending the F20's protest activity. Islamists coming into power following the 2011 MENA Uprisings were often viewed as a threat to the state. In Morocco, however, the winning of the PJD in parliamentary elections signaled to the public that change had occurred and convinced many Moroccans that a social movement for change was no longer needed. In essence, the state needed the Islamists to win. This scenario explains why the PJD victory in the general elections of 2011 is called by activists the "regime's last card."

Chapter 5 builds a theory on how movement structure modulates interorganizational trust, which can significantly influence the success or decline of a movement. I first review the history of violence within Moroccan universities, which demonstrates the long-standing ideological contention between leftists and Islamists in Morocco. I then use interview narratives to explain how cross-ideological cooperation between Islamists and Communists was the most controversial alliance within the F20. This alliance made many leftists uncomfortable with joining forces with what they viewed as an enemy. This cooperation led to controversy and internal fractures within the F20 throughout the country, but it also led to internal perceptions of movement co-optation by what many leftists viewed as extremists. The case of the F20 suggests that within ideologically and politically heterogenous movements, a lack of structure and hierarchy is a facilitator of movement decline. The lack of structure and hierarchy in decision making allowed internal divides to occur and perceptions that ideological competitors were "hijacking the movement" to permeate.

Chapter 6 covers the various implications for future research specific to Morocco and social movement theory in general. Considering recent waves of protest in the restive Rif region of Morocco concerning police brutality and corruption, previous F20 members are mobilizing again throughout the country to support Riffians. Social movement scholars find that increased contact among different groups will increase the likelihood of increased cooperation and coalitions. According to interviewees, the F20 movement changed Moroccan politics and started a new "culture of street protests," like the Hirak-al-Rif movement.

1

Demobilization

A Theory and Lessons from the Field

At the height of the F20's activity, hundreds of thousands took part in protests (Emiljanowicz 2017). The interaction between tech-savvy e-activists and street activists inspired by the events in Tunisia and Egypt is credited with founding the F20 (Rachidi 2015). Before the movement started, there were various online calls for protests by unconnected individuals. The first official and well-known call for protest by the F20 was a successful online video that promoted protests for a myriad of reasons, including calls for more freedoms and minority rights. The video first appeared on YouTube and begins with a woman telling viewers that "I am Moroccan, and I will march on February 20th because I want freedom and equality for all Moroccans."[1] The video is an amalgamation of men and women expressing why they will join the protest movement. The Moroccan Association for Human Rights (AMDH), the largest human rights nongovernmental organization (NGO) in Morocco, provided the space and filming equipment for the video and convinced young activists to create the video. Moreover, AMDH invited all individuals and political organizations that were interested in change to join protests on February 20, 2011.[2]

The founders were leftist leaning and not religiously affiliated. Similarly, the movement's official webpage, Mamfakinch, makes it appear that the F20 is leftist and secular; opinion articles deride the privatization of

1. Video found at https://www.youtube.com/watch?v=S0f6FSB7gxQ.
2. AMDH leader, interview with the author, Oct. 5, 2016, Rabat.

industries and the incumbent Islamist ruling party.[3] However, Islamist, leftist, feminist, liberal, and Amazigh (Berber) elements—all of which have competing views on the aforementioned issues—participated under its banner. Furthermore, although the F20 was a collective of various individual activists, it was supported by many political parties and organizations. The main non-Islamic political parties that supported the movement were radical left-wing parties like the United Socialist Party (USP) and the Marxist Democratic Way Party (DWP). Other organizations like the Moroccan Association of Human Rights and the Amazigh Democracy Movement also supported the F20.

The most notable political parties and organizations of the F20 were the Islamist Justice and Charity Organization (JCO) along with the USP and the DWP. The JCO is officially an illegal organization, but it is largely tolerated within Morocco. Its late founder, Abdessalam Yassine, infused the hierarchical structure of Sufism, with the goal of transforming Morocco into an Islamist state. Indeed, the JCO "operates like a social movement by providing services and assistance to the poorer sections of society and which is preoccupied with Islamizing society from below by promoting a sort of Sufi-infused utopianism" (Dalmasso 2012, 222). The JCO was the largest Islamist organization to join the F20; however, other smaller Islamist organizations did join as well, most notably Hizb al-Umma (Party of the Nation), which situates its ideological identity between Islamism and liberalism. In the words of one member: "Hizb al-Umma was quite in the middle. It tried to unify the JCO's quantity [foot power] and the leftist's quality [ideology]."[4] One leftist activist jokingly labeled Hizb al-Umma as "nearly leftists" and claimed that "they were closer to the Left than the Islamists." The same activist claims it was because Hizb al-Umma "practiced 'secular Islam,' in parenthesis, they say that I have no right to change your religion, you can be Muslim or practice another religion because it [religion] is a personal issue."[5] The party was founded in 2007 and is inspired by Islamic principles while fighting

3. See https://www.mamfakinch.com/.
4. Hizb al-Umma member, interview by the author, Nov. 15, 2016, Meknes.
5. CDT MP, interview by the author, Jan. 13, 2017, Rabat.

against ethnic, religious, linguistic, and gender discrimination. It maintains good relationships with leftist parties and, like the JCO, is an illegal but tolerated political organization.

Unlike political organizations, labor unions played a minimal role in F20 protests. In Tunisia, the Tunisian General Labor Union (UGTT) was very active in street protests during the 2011 MENA Uprisings, but labor-union involvement with the F20 was weak. Moroccan labor unions, most significantly the Moroccan Workers Union (UMT), ceased supporting the F20 in April 2011, a month after unprecedented constitutional reforms and early elections were declared, since higher salaries for civil servants were implemented (Rachidi 2015). In Morocco, unions like the UMT used the 2011 MENA Uprisings to enhance their material interests (Buehler 2015). Initially, Moroccan labor unions supported street protests, but, following state-labor negotiations in April 2011, the state conceded to union demands, which included raising the private-sector minimum wage by 330 dirhams ($33) and public-sector wages by 600 dirhams ($60). Matt Buehler argues that Moroccan labor unions, therefore, utilized the 2011 MENA Uprisings for their own interests: "These concessions show that public employees—teachers, doctors, nurses, and government clerks—emerged as victors from Morocco's Arab uprising of 2011. Afraid that sustained labour participation in protests could provoke urban riots, as it frequently had between the 1930s and 2000s, the regime acquiesced to calm syndicate anger" (2015, 102).

Unlike the UMT, the political parties and human rights organizations involved with the F20 overwhelmingly rejected the announcement of constitutional reforms; however, the Socialist Union of Popular Forces (USFP) did decide to officially withdraw support from the F20 following constitutional reforms. This decision did not come as a surprise to many, as the USFP was the only party within the F20 that had previously held a parliamentary plurality (1997, 2002) and also therefore a long history of fighting for change within government institutions. Although the F20 rejected the reforms announced on March 9, 2011, many Moroccans rejoiced. Following the speech, the F20 was confronted with a dilemma it could never adequately overcome: How does a movement convince a public that is overwhelmingly supportive of the king to join F20 protests?

The Reformist King

The Moroccan regime's initial response to F20 protests was to offer various major concessions. However, concessions did not independently quell protests in Morocco. Repression was less frequently used by the Moroccan regime and was, like concessions, not sufficient to lead to demobilization alone. When direct repression aimed at immediately dispersing protests was used in Morocco, it occurred months after protests began in May 2011. During May, activists began changing tactics by protesting in "nonpublic areas," like popular neighborhoods.

Following three weeks of nationwide demonstrations, King Mohammed VI addressed Moroccans via televised broadcast on March 9, 2011. To the surprise of many, the king announced sweeping constitutional reforms that reduced the monarch's power and called for early elections. Various scholars have posited that these reforms were the main factor leading to abatement of the protests in Morocco (Yom and Gause 2012; Amar and Prashad 2013; Lynch 2013). Without specifically mentioning the F20, the king announced that he would appoint a commission to ensure a separation of powers between the monarch, the judiciary, and the legislature. Perhaps the most important proposal was permitting freer parliamentary elections. The king would no longer limit the number of seats allocated to a party, which allowed the Islamist Party of Justice and Development to win a plurality of seats in the 2011 general election (Abend 2011). As we will see, activists quickly made it clear that the parliamentary victory of the PJD in 2011 played a major role in reducing protests, which is why the PJD victory is termed by interviewees as the "regime's last card." The PJD victory further convinced the public and some F20 activists that sufficient change had occurred and that street protests were no longer necessary. Islamists within the F20 left the movement within two weeks of the PJD victory. This departure was viewed by activists as the most palpable blow to the movement and was preceded by internal conflicts between Islamists and leftists concerning the future of the F20.

In addition to the constitutional reforms, the king pardoned various human rights activists and ultraconservative Islamist-Salafists, some of whom were arrested following the 2003 Casablanca terrorist attacks (Arieff

Table 1

2011 Concessions

February 21, 2011	Former prime minister Abbas el-Fassi announced that negotiations between the state and labor organizations would be initiated
March 9, 2011	The king announced the formation of a constitutional reform committee
April 9, 2011	Abbas el-Fassi drafted concessions for labor unions
April 14, 2011	The king pardoned 148 political prisoners
April 26, 2011	Unprecedented increases in minimum wage and retirement pensions were passed and accepted by labor unions
June 17, 2011	New constitution was presented to the public
July 1, 2011	New constitution passed via referendum vote
November 25, 2011	Early free and fair elections were held, which resulted in a plurality for the Islamist PJD

2013, 5). Following a popular referendum vote, the sweeping reforms were passed in July 2011. The government claims that voter turnout was just over 70 percent and that 98 percent voted yes to passing the new constitution (National Democratic Institute 2011). Table 1 chronologically outlines concessions made by the monarchy during 2011.

King Mohammed VI has historically responded to grievances from civil society via reforms. The passing of the Moroccan Family Law Code known as the Mudawwana in 2004, which was proposed to the parliament by King Mohammed VI, was praised by the international community and was the result of more than "20 years of struggle by feminists and women's NGOs" (Ennaji 2016, 103, 85). Feather notes that prior to the passing of the new Mudawwana, "more than 60 women's groups organized demonstrations in Rabat calling for reforms to women's legal status, especially within the family code," while Islamist organizations held rallies opposing such reform (2014, 22). The new code conceded to key feminist demands like raising the age of marriage to eighteen for both sexes, allowing polygamy only with the first wife's consent, allowing women to file for divorce, officially recognizing and registering children born outside of wedlock, and allowing both spouses to be responsible for the family. Essentially, the new Mudawwana has paved the path toward more gender equality and is one of the most progressive examples of women's rights legislation in the region.

Similarly, King Mohammed VI created a truth and reconciliation committee (Instance Équité et Réconciliation) in response to reports of human rights atrocities against dissidents throughout his father's (King Hassan II) reign in the 1960s and 1980s, a period that is referred to in Morocco as the "Years of Lead." Human Rights Watch hailed the reconciliation committee as an "unprecedented development" in the MENA region and as "proof of the country's commitment to political reform."[6] This reformist trend of the monarchy has "granted the regime a reputation of being on the road to democratization" (Dalmasso 2012, 219).

Although many activists portray the reforms of 2011 as merely cosmetic, the reforms were unprecedented. The reforms give more power to parliament and the prime minister, who is now appointed by the king from the largest party in the Moroccan parliament. Furthermore, the reforms give "more independence to the judiciary, more protection of human rights and recognition of the Moroccan cultural diversity as well as the Amazigh language as the second official language of the country" (Laachir 2012). Nevertheless, significant power remains with the king; for instance, he appointed the committee to draft a new constitution, and the new constitution does not affect the king's control of security and foreign policy issues.[7]

Despite the significance of the reforms, the F20's protests increased following the initial declaration of reforms on March 9, 2011. On March

6. "Morocco's Truth Commission Honoring Past Victims during an Uncertain Present," Human Rights Watch, https://www.hrw.org/sites/default/files/reports/morocco1105wcover.pdf.
7. "Morocco's Truth Commission Honoring Past Victims."

13, 2011, there were protests in Casablanca that were violently repressed, and one of the largest protests organized by the F20 occurred on March 20, 2011, when tens of thousands protested throughout Morocco in rejection of the king's speech.[8] In the words of one AMDH leader: "The Moroccan people want something that goes beyond the king's speech." In the capital city of Rabat and in Casablanca, slogans turned more extreme with crowds chanting "The people want to overthrow the tyranny," with fifty thousand participating in Casablanca alone.[9] Protests were not limited to big cities, however. Cities like Taza, Safi, Al-Hoceima, Nador, and Ouarzazate all had major protests on March 20. The months of March and April continued to see weekly protests that were often met with repression. In essence, the F20's rejection of the March 9 speech was clear. Indeed, a leader within the JCO made it clear that the March 9 speech may have even strengthened the movement: "The state thought that after the king's speech, protests would stop or weaken and recede, but the opposite occurred. The marches that occurred in April and May were the strongest marches."[10] Other activists believed that the proposed constitutional referendum following the March 9 speech created an opportunity for the F20 to unite behind the decision of boycotting the constitution.[11] As we will see, however, targeted repression and implementation of reforms would eventually convince some within the movement to abandon street protests.

The events in Morocco question conventional wisdom that links concessions or repression, individually, to the lessening of protests. The Moroccan monarchy's strategy of concessions and repression, together, helped quell protests in Morocco. I will show how this mixed policy was incredibly effective in demobilizing the F20. In the next section, I outline the findings from the broader social movement and authoritarian persistence literature and what this book adds to that literature.

8. "Thousands of Moroccans Demand Change, End to Corruption," Alarabiya, Mar. 20, 2011, https://www.alarabiya.net/articles/2011%2F03%2F20%2F142313.

9. "Tens of Thousands in the Rallies of Rabat, Al-Bayda, Fez and Others This Morning," Maghress, Mar. 20, 2011, https://www.maghress.com/arrifinu/38457.

10. JCO leader, interview by the author, Oct. 31, 2016, Rabat.

11. Talea member, interview by the author, Dec. 8, 2016, Rabat.

Social Movement Theory and Demobilization

Social movement and protest literature more generally has focused almost exclusively on the relationship between repression and protest (see Lichbach 1987; Whalen and Flacks 1989; Mason and Krane 1989; Francisco 1995, 2004; Gupta, Singh, and Sprague 1993; and Linden and Klandermans 2006). The well-studied causal relationship between repression and protest levels reveals that the level of repression matters; for instance, if repression is harsh, then it will likely reduce backlash protests and lead to eventual demobilization (Francisco 2004; Pierskalla 2010). Sometimes, the transmission of images of harsh repression deters others from protesting. For example, Harris (2012) uses the case study of the 2009 Iranian Green Movement to argue that images of harsh repression shared online, in part, led to that movement's demobilization by convincing people the costs of protesting were too high.

A widely accepted finding concerning reforms and concessions[12] in relation to protest levels is Mark Lichbach's finding that consistent concessions or reforms lead to protest abatement. Lichbach's seminal analysis of the relationship between repression and dissent argues that dissent varies with the consistency of state policy. In other words, consistent government repressive or accommodative policies (like reforms) will reduce dissent, while inconsistent policies will increase it. His inadvertent advice for governments is "Don't reward and punish the same tactic" (1987, 287). Said differently, accommodate or repress dissenters, but don't mix. The Moroccan case is one where reforms and other concessionary policies were the main policy of the regime in response to protests; however, after each concession, repression followed. The Moroccan case demonstrates that, despite consistent accommodative policies, protests did not immediately abate. It also demonstrates how a mixed governmental policy of concessions followed by repression led to demobilization.

Mark Lichbach's question is "how repression both escalates and deters dissent" (1987, 271). Similarly, I show that accommodative policies can similarly escalate or deter dissent. Overlooked and crucial determinants

---

12. Lichbach uses the term *accommodative policies*.

of this relationship are sequence, the agents involved (that is, homogenous or heterogeneous movements), type of concession (unprecedented or familiar), and type and aim of repression (harsh crackdowns or targeted defamation campaigns). After initial concessions in March 2011, the Moroccan regime responded to protests with a mixed policy of concessions and repression. This mixture suggests that neither concessions nor repression was independently sufficient to quell protests. Rather, I argue reforms did not directly convince F20 activists to cease protests; rather, initial reforms initiated internal disputes and cleavages that incrementally divided a previously united movement. As I will discuss, repressive tactics further divided the movement and convinced the public that the costs of protesting (while change was already occurring) were too high.

Authoritarian Persistence

Regimes in the MENA have been apt at co-opting opposition and using regime-backed parties to consolidate power (Yom and Gause 2012; Albrecht 2005; Maghraoui 2011; Buehler 2015). Elections and the inclusion of Islamist opposition parties into the formal political process have also led to authoritarian persistence (Brownlee 2007; Blaydes 2010; Wegner 2011). Moreover, where civil society has blossomed, authoritarian regimes have managed to reassert their grip on power (Zartman 1988). For instance, Cavatorta (2009) finds that a vibrant civil society in Morocco has actually strengthened the king's power. Focusing on the reformed internationally praised Family Code Law, the Mudawwana, Cavatorta finds that the king was effectively able to use direct decision-making power to control the reform process and present himself as a defender of women's rights. In essence, he took credit for the work of Moroccan civil society that pushed for reforms to the Family Code Law since the 1990s. Brumberg (2002, 2013) outlines how liberalized autocracies, like Morocco, rely on state-managed pluralism and can simultaneously allow competing civil society groups to function while also effectively playing one group against another (2013, 91). Brumberg (2002) highlights how liberalized autocrats can control elections, while also selectively repressing opposition when the regime is threatened.

Regional events are also important. Alrababa'h and Blaydes (2021) make the case that leaders engage in diversionary conflicts to turn the public's attention away from domestic problems. Similarly, social learning can occur among regimes and lead to "authoritarian resilience" (Heydemann and Leenders 2011). During the 2011 MENA Uprisings, regimes learned from each other to effectively demobilize protests. Prior to the outbreak of protests in Morocco, the regime witnessed how failed repressive policies of the Tunisian and Egyptian autocrats led to regime change. Other leaders also recognized that relying purely on repression would backfire. For instance, President Ali Abdullah Saleh of Yemen unsuccessfully tried to remain in power by offering promising elections and not running for office, while Bashar al-Assad of Syria failed to abate protests after announcing political reforms. The distinction in the Moroccan case is that unlike Syria or Yemen, the Moroccan king did not renege on past announcements of reform. We will see how past policies matter and highlight why reforms effectively quell dissent in some contexts but not others.

The Moroccan case highlights how authoritarians without great rentier resources can outmaneuver social movements and quell dissent without relying exclusively on repression. This book adds to the established literature that highlights how authoritarian regimes in the MENA are flexible and adapt to environmental changes in important ways (Blaydes 2010, 8). Stacher highlights how autocrats adapt to environmental changes by implementing carefully managed reforms to "maintain their dominant position and hierarchical authority over society" (2012, 21). Within this analysis, how centralized or dispersed institutional power is important. In other words, the more centralized power is with the executive, the more efficiently they can adapt (implement reforms) in order to maintain authority. In Morocco, power is centralized with the monarch, and he can effectively adapt to environmental changes through mandating reforms. This book complements the authoritarian persistence literature by demonstrating how the king's reformist past and general popularity serve as opportunities to quell dissent and consolidate power. Moreover, we will see how an Islamist opposition party can be used by the regime to quell dissent and further abate protests.

To understand Morocco's regime persistence in light of the 2011 MENA Uprisings, I investigate what effects democratic changes and repression have had on the internal dynamics of the F20. In other words, the book builds on the existing authoritarian persistence literature and incorporates social movement analysis in order to understand how dissent is quelled and authoritarians maintain power. This point is important since, as demonstrated by the 2011 MENA Uprisings, the 2018 Sudanese Revolution, the Lebanese October Revolution, and the 2019 Algerian Revolution of Smiles, social movements can quickly threaten and dispose of long-standing autocrats. Said differently, this book investigates social movement dynamics in order to better understand authoritarian persistence. The next section outlines my theory of how accommodation followed by repression effectively abates dissent and ultimately authoritarian persistence.

Concessions and Repression: A Theory

Signals sent to a public about the legitimacy and necessity of a social movement affect whether bystanders will join or cease participation. This dynamic not only refers to the size of protests but also refers to whether the movement aligns with public opinion (that is, if they are perceived as moderate and not extremist). Timur Kuran's (1989, 1991) theory of "falsified preferences" contends that bystanders join protests when "first movers" signal to society that they share their grievances. Depending on environmental factors, like how the regime reacts, more or less of society will join. For instance, if protesters are not repressed, then more bystanders who share the same grievances with first movers will begin to mobilize. Kuran's theory of preference falsification distinguishes between private and public preferences. For example, within an authoritarian context, private opinion about the regime will differ from public preferences because expressing negative opinions toward the regime may lead to punishment.

Lohmann builds on Kuran's theory and shows that "people's incentives to participate depend on their expectations about how many others will turn out, and they revise their beliefs based on changes in turnout over time" (1994, 50). Lohmann adds to the signaling model by showing that the propensity for the public to protest depends on "informational cues from changes in size of the protest movement over time" (49). Moreover, Lohmann finds that demonstrations will attract greater support when more moderates, and not solely extremists, make up protests. The signals sent to Moroccan society through state propaganda campaigns (including a referendum and election campaign) and the F20 itself (primarily via slogans and banners) eventually led to the perception by society that the F20 was dominated by radical organizations and no longer needed since democratic changes were being implemented through a king who is widely accepted as legitimate.

I offer a theory that demonstrates how "mixed policy" (accommodation followed by repression) abates dissent when there is a history of implementation of reforms, there is a conveyance by power holders (signals) of addressing grievances through unprecedented concessions, and there is an increasing disunity between a public's and a social movement's perceived goals. Therefore, for accommodative/repressive policies to work, there need not be a consistency of sticking to one policy (reforms or repression). A calculated mixed-policy approach aims to demobilize a social movement by delegitimizing it, in addition to internally fracturing it. Therefore, one tactic undertaken by the regime is to convince the general public that the F20's persistence is no longer needed. This persuasion is accomplished by systematically offering reforms that address specific social movement grievances. The other is highlighting internal cleavages within the F20, which, as this book demonstrates, was successful. It was accomplished by smearing the F20 as composed of Islamist fundamentalists and labeling secular leftists as anti-Islamic. This framing of the movement is critical in Morocco where the role of Islam in politics is overwhelmingly controlled by the palace. The king is *amir almouminin* (commander of the faithful), which grants him complete guardianship and control over religion. Therefore, this smear campaign highlighted differences between leftists and Islamists and caused internal conflicts.[13] In essence, concessionary policies convinced society that demands were being met and therefore led to the perception that the F20 was no longer needed, while repression highlighted further internal divides.

To illustrate, in figure 1, I propose that there are two trajectories to protest demobilization. The first, seen on the upper pathway, is a familiar

---

13. Direct repression was used only after the F20's grievances were met with concessions.

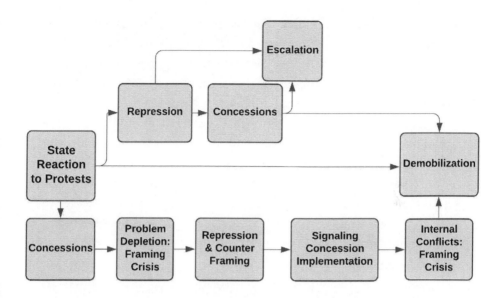

trajectory that most countries within the 2011 MENA Uprisings followed. The initial state reaction was usually repression, often followed by concessions and more cycles of repression.

What I suggest is that the processes that led to divergent paths to demobilization found in figure 1 depend on the characteristics of the agents involved. For example, heterogeneous social movements are more prone to fracture following government policies like repression. Moreover, reneging on past promises of reform will likely not convince a public that new concessions will be implemented. For instance, the cases of Syria and Egypt demonstrate how repression followed by promises of concessions led to cycles of escalation and violence. As indicated in figure 1, a history of declaring and implementing reforms is needed for concessions to demobilize a movement. This precedent was not the case in Yemen. Although President Saleh responded first with familiar concessions and then harsh repression, he also reneged on a 2006 promise to not seek reelection. President Saleh promised economic reforms, early parliamentary and presidential elections, and not to run for reelection. However, concessions following mass protests in 2011 did not de-escalate protests and lead to demobilization (Gasim 2014, 128). Said differently, a public will not likely believe a leader who has previously announced reforms but failed to go through with them. Like in Syria, the Yemeni president's previous bluff of announcing, but not implementing, reforms sent a clear signal to the public that announcements of concessions do not necessarily mean they will be implemented.

I argue that a popular leader who has a track record of declaring and implementing reforms will more likely find that the announcement of concessions will persuade the public and will not be viewed as bluffs. As we have seen, King Mohammed VI has been viewed as a reformist. Said differently, since the king has historically implemented reforms in response to grievances, the public had strong reasons to believe the promises of reform declared on March 9, 2011, would be implemented.

The second, lower, trajectory in figure 1 outlines how Moroccan protests demobilized. The Moroccan regime's initial response to protests during the 2011 MENA Uprisings was to consistently and strategically offer and implement unprecedented concessionary policies, which signaled to the public that significant change was occurring and that the social movement's demands were being met. The regime's reforms are strategic since different concessions have been directed at specific groups' requests and grievances. For example, the Amazigh Cultural Movement's demand of cultural recognition was met with a constitutional amendment that made Tamazight, the Amazigh national language, an official language. The king took a similar approach with labor unions, which were hesitant to give their full support to the F20. To ensure that labor unions would not become heavily involved with F20 protests, state-labor negotiations were announced a day after protests started on February 21, 2011. These extensive state-union negotiations led to concessions that conceded to nearly all the demands of the labor unions. Similarly, on April 14, 2011, the king pardoned Salafist political prisoners, which was the main demand of Salafist supporters of the F20. The regime's strategy of granting certain groups precisely their demands in order to lessen the presence of some activists from the streets worked. In the view of many within the public, the king's concessionary policies were an indication that the F20's demands would also be met. Moreover, the regime signaled to the public that reforms were being actively implemented, primarily through the 2011 Referendum Campaign, further disincentivizing street politics.

Public perception of initial demands being met forces social movements to experiment with different frames to address and solve the perceived problem depletion. We will see that after the regime's mixed policy, the F20 focused on whether and how to change tactics or frames to attract public support. In other words, the regime's concessions and repression internally fractured the movement since it no longer had one united frame but instead had divergent ones—some explicitly revolutionary. In a context where leftists (often Marxists) are Islamic but not Islamist, the role of Islamic symbols and chants becomes an especially contentious issue within social movements. How the F20 was framed both internally (by different Islamist, leftist, and secularist organizations) and externally (by the state) had a profound impact on the internal social movement dynamics and resonance with the public. Similarly, movement structure and composition can be an important factor in determining how movements are affected by reforms or repression. Some movements are inherently more prone to fracturing, which is exacerbated by the effect of reforms and repression. If a movement is composed of various loosely connected organizations with low trust levels, they will likely continue to deteriorate. Inversely, if a movement is highly homogenous and trust among members is high, then trust levels will more likely remain stable. We will see that how the F20 was framed to the general public was of constant concern to the movement and that issues concerning how to strategically frame the movement became more frequent following concessions and repression by the state.

Repression, within this context, can further alienate the movement from the public and also convince activists to leave the movement. As mentioned, repressing a movement when it is popular with the public may immediately quell protests, but can also lead to increased support for the social movement as well as increased long-term dissent. Nonetheless, repressing a movement that the public perceives as "crossing red lines" or as radical, or both, will more likely be viewed as justified by the public (Koopmans 2005). Moreover, interviewees made clear that direct repression further disincentivized activists from continuing to protest. As we will see, this logic explains why harsh repression was used roughly three months after protests began and when the movement was already becoming alienated from the public.

Lessons from the Field

Political groups in Morocco tend to label themselves as either leftist, Islamist, or cultural movements. I interviewed fifteen participants from self-described Islamist parties (JCO and Hizb al-Umma), eleven are from leftist parties (USP, Democratic Way Party, Talea, USFP), ten independent F20 activists that did not represent political parties, three members from the Amazigh movement, and one member from the Alternative Movement for Personal Liberties (MALI). Additionally, I interviewed three members from the Democratic Confederation of Labor (CDT), all of whom were active members in leftist parties, and one regional leader from the Moroccan Workers' Union who was also a member in Hizb al-Umma. Finally, all interviewees from the Moroccan Association for Human Rights are active members of the Democratic Way Party.

The interviews gathered descriptive information as well as information concerning participants' ideological beliefs, affiliations, and positions within various organizations. This basic information helped me decipher different ideological affiliations within the F20. My open-ended questions were aimed at letting interviewees elaborate on whether ideological divides existed and became highlighted at some point and how internal and external events (that is, reforms/regional conflicts) affected the movement (see Kvale 2008; Taber 2010; and Rubin and Rubin 2011). The interview questions were designed to gather data that would elucidate the reasons behind the breakup of the F20 and its abatement of contentious activity.

Although the F20 is a leaderless movement, organizations and parties operating within this movement do have organizational leaders and elites, and my interview sample included many of these leaders. Since the main ideological divide in the F20 was between Islamist and leftists, I interviewed a representative sample of various members and party leaders of the JCO. Similarly, I conducted interviews with all the main leftist organizations that participated in the F20. Some groups do not fall into a leftist/Islamist dichotomy, like the Cultural (Berber) Amazigh movement. I also interviewed elites from the Amazigh movement to better gain insights outside of the main leftist and Islamist camps within the movement. These interviews provide insights into the relationship between reforms and demobilization.

Ethics and Identity

Feminist researchers have struggled with the issue of representing oneself and the implications that identity has on field research (Daniels 1983; Wolf 2019). Some scholars have argued that researchers who are from the areas where they conduct fieldwork are better positioned to understand "emotive dimensions of behavior" (Ohnuki-Tierney 1984, 584). Other scholars, like Lila Abu-Lughod (1991), argue that "halfie positionality" leads to different relationships and power dynamics with research participants. Less research has been conducted about how some ethnic backgrounds within certain contexts may open doors (that is, gaining access to interviewees) while simultaneously risking closing them. In other words, some researchers need to be especially careful with how to represent themselves in the field.

In Morocco, I quickly learned how important the Palestinian quest for independence and human rights is for Moroccans. Researchers have written about the dilemmas and advantages of having a similar or same ethnic background with their interviewees. However, I do not consider myself to be a native or "halfie" within Morocco and the greater Maghreb region. Within Morocco, a context where both Amazigh (Berber), European, and Arab cultures influence modern Moroccan national culture, I cannot claim to be intimately tied to the country's inhabitants on grounds of being of Arab descent. Nevertheless, as a researcher of Palestinian descent, I argue that my identity did facilitate access to closed networks of interviewees, while also creating methodological dilemmas.

An adage I was repeatedly told by interviewees was "In Morocco, the Palestinian issue is a national issue." Indeed, one of the largest demonstrations in Morocco in 2012 was a solidarity protest for Palestine that amassed one hundred thousand demonstrators in Rabat.[14] In other words, it is a personal issue for many Moroccans, and especially politically active Moroccans. Mass mobilizations in support of Palestinian liberation are common in Morocco with parties across all ideologies. Most recently, tens of thousands protested the US decision to move the US embassy to Jerusalem.[15] Therefore, researchers who are ethnically tied to the Palestinian-Israeli conflict will face unique methodological dilemmas within Morocco and, I suspect, the Maghreb region. The importance of this issue to interviewees in Morocco leads to the opening of doors along with the creation of certain methodological dilemmas. This research uses field notes written shortly after interviews and builds on previous literature by considering how some ethnic identities tied to politically sensitive issues (in this case the Palestinian-Israeli conflict) may lead to ethical dilemmas and how future researchers in similar situations can negotiate such quandaries.

Open Doors

During my first month of fieldwork in Morocco, I introduced myself to interviewees as an American researcher who was investigating social movement dynamics within Morocco. Interviewees almost unanimously inquired about my last name and my ethnic background and nearly exclusively began referring to me either as a Palestinian or as a "Palestinian from America." Upon identifying as an American of Palestinian decent, getting access to elites within the F20 became easier. In other words, although I do not have familial ties to Morocco, getting access to otherwise closed networks was possible in large part owing to my ethnic background. Many interviewees asked about my last name, and I soon learned that my ethnicity would serve as a "rite of passage" into networks of activists that I thought would be more difficult to reach. In the words of one activist: "We treat Palestinians in a special way here."

14. "Nearly 100,000 Participants Marched in Support of Al Quds Al Sharif in Rabat," *Hespress*, Mar. 25, 2012, https://www.hespress.com/politique/50277.html.

15. "Tens of Thousands Rally in Morocco against US Jerusalem Move," *Times of Israel*, Dec. 10, 2017, https://www.timesofisrael.com/tens-of-thousands-rally-in-morocco-against-us-jerusalem-move/.

In October 2011, I began interviewing members of a Marxist political party called the Democratic Way Party. The DWP is directly tied with Morocco's largest human rights organization, the Moroccan Association of Human Rights, as all AMDH members I interviewed were also DWP members. I interviewed two AMDH members at their offices in Rabat who provided me with elite contacts within the F20. DWP activists made it clear that they connected me with various movement leaders because of my ethnic background. In one instance, an interviewee indicated that since I was Palestinian, he would provide me with an important contact. After an interview with an activist in a café, the interviewee introduced me to a cofounder of the F20 who said, "Oh, you are the Palestinian researcher!" I soon realized that my identity facilitated the daunting task of getting interviews through chain-of-referral sampling. In one instance, a member of the illegal Islamist organization, the Justice and Charity Organization, was happy to set up an interview and referred to me as the "Palestinian studying in America." Was it unethical to not correct the interviewee? Should I have emphasized that I was an American of Palestinian descent? Would downplaying my Palestinian ethnicity while highlighting my American nationality have angered some interviewees? These questions led to some ethical dilemmas.

Closed Doors

Interviewees almost unanimously focused on my Palestinian heritage, while downplaying or ignoring my American nationality. Interviewees usually knew that I was not directly from the region—either through my directly informing them or via inference through my imperfect Shamy (Levantine) Arabic. Nevertheless, my Palestinian identity always overshadowed my Americanness. In one case, an interviewee took issue with my using the term *Palestinian American* and instructed me that I was not American, but solely Palestinian. Inversely, in another case, an elder activist took issue with my self-identification as Palestinian American after asking me if I financially assisted the Palestinian cause. I hesitated and was taken aback by this question and did not answer. The interviewee quickly balked: "Then you are not Palestinian." Another interviewee who was with the elder interviewee noticed the awkward situation I was placed in and apologized. Following this incident, I realized that even though I felt that my identity opened many doors in terms of access to interviewees, it was also a slippery slope that I would need to carefully manage.

A similar situation occurred toward the end of an interview with an Islamist activist in Casablanca. The interviewee expectedly inquired about my ethnic background and asked me about the Palestinian-Israeli issue from the "perspective of a Palestinian American." Among other things, I informed the interviewee that I personally did not have a lot of hope for Palestinian statehood in the near future. The interviewee was visibly upset with this response, and, in his words, was troubled to hear a "a child of Palestine says this." The interviewee expressed how important Palestinian statehood was for all Moroccans and that only with "Islam and unity" can statehood be achieved. He made it clear that he "has hope for Palestinian liberation" and that I—as a Palestinian American—should feel the same way. This conversation occurred at the end and not the beginning of the interview, and the interviewee did not offer to provide me with further contacts for interviews. Therefore, simply saying that I had little hope for Palestinian statehood in the near future—as a Palestinian American— seemed to offend this interviewee and perhaps could have closed doors that were previously open.

Lunch with Syndicates

I called the Democratic Confederation of Labor headquarters in Casablan-ca.[16] After gathering my contact information, I received a call the same day and was invited to meet with various elite syndicates at CDT headquarters in Casablanca. Upon entering the CDT offices, I saw banners and posters for various political causes and leaders, the most prevalent being support for the Palestinian cause. This passage from my field notes illustrates how important the Palestinian issue was for the CDT: "I was greeted by a CDT leader and was led to a conference room. In the conference rooms there were political posters and stickers supporting Palestine—even the wall

---

16. The CDT is a socialist labor union that was closely aligned with the F20.

clock had a Palestinian flag on it."[17] The CDT interviewees tended to be interested in both my Palestinian and my American identities, and conversations ranged from issues concerning Moroccan politics, the impending Trump presidency at the time, and of course Palestine.

After interviewing a CDT elite, I was invited to have lunch with all of the union members. Among the political posters plastered on concrete walls, I noticed Palestinian flags and an especially large framed poster of the late Palestinian Liberation Organization leader Yasser Arafat in the union cafeteria. I was introduced to everyone at the table as a "Palestinian from America." In the midst of conversations, I knew that I was generously allowed to share a meal in the CDT's cafeteria for employees (and introduced to various elite CDT syndicates) because of my ethnic background. I felt most nervous when directly questioned by some at the lunch table about my dedication to the Palestinian cause.

Among the conversations we had was one about Palestinians in the United States and their lack of building powerful lobbies for Palestinian statehood.[18] An elite CDT member asked me why as Palestinians in America we do not form lobbies to help Palestine and whether I identify politically more with Palestine or America. I was very careful when answering these questions since I could not ethically claim to be an activist or a lobbyist. This passage from my field notes demonstrates how researchers with certain ethnic backgrounds may need to prepare answers to questions they may have otherwise not thought about: "I am realizing that I have to carefully answer such questions and be careful not to jeopardize losing an interview. For example, having a ready response to the question about Palestinian lobbies would be helpful. These pre-interview discussions, I believe, can really affect whether you get access to people and what the tone of the interview will be like. The Palestinian issue is very important to the CDT, and I was treated specially because of my ethnicity."

17. CDT leader, interview by the author, Jan. 19, 2017, Casablanca.
18. The American Israel Public Affair Committee (AIPAC) was referenced as an example.

After four months of interviews in Morocco, I became accustomed to and expected questions concerning my identity. More often than not, research participants would informally interview me when I concluded my questions. There was an expectation among interviewees that, as a person of Palestinian descent, I must be an activist for Palestinian statehood.

Essentially, some identities carry with them political expectations within certain contexts. I imagine that Jewish American researchers within the MENA may face an inverse dilemma of having to separate their Jewish identity from Zionist ideology. Before future researchers in similar situations conduct fieldwork, I suggest clarifying how to present the researcher's identity and contemplating how to answer questions about the researcher's connection to politically sensitive and important issues. There may be an expectation to be more intimately tied to certain issues based on the researcher's identity; therefore, being knowledgeable of the issue and understanding the importance of said issue to research participants is critical and may have implications for the overall success of fieldwork.

Conclusion

Gaining access to closed activist networks is what informs the findings of this book. The following chapters delve into interviews with activists throughout Morocco to show how the F20 was demobilized. My interviews reveal how historically antagonistic activist networks initially unite and eventually become divided. We will see why, after reforms were announced, the F20's message became less attractive to the general public and reformist activists alike.

2

Concessions

Giving the Movement What They Want

On March 9, 2011, King Mohammed VI responded to the F20's demands via a televised address. The king started the speech by indicating that new constitutional reforms would further the country's "model of democracy and development."[1] The speech categorically addressed the movement's demands, like devolving some of the king's powers, ending corruption, and recognizing the Amazigh language. For the first time in fifteen years, the constitution would be reformed—another key demand of the F20. Many Moroccans rejoiced and celebrated the speech. The F20, however, faced an existential crisis and rejected the speech as cosmetic. In the words of one elite activist: "There was a general opinion [within the F20] that the constitution is not democratic and does not adequately divide powers."[2] Nevertheless, according to the public, the king offered the F20 precisely what they were demanding; why continue protesting?

As we will see, the announcement of major reforms was an existential threat to the F20. The movement responded to this threat by experimenting with frames to test resonance with the public. Framing concerns how organizations, individuals, and even governments socially construct and portray reality. For frames to resonate with a public, they need to be culturally compatible, consistent, and relevant to the target audience (Johnston and Noakes 2005, 15). The problem, however, is that the F20 was not united

---

1. "Morocco's King Mohammed Pledges Constitutional Reform," BBC, Mar. 9, 2011, https://www.bbc.co.uk/news/world-africa-12695092.

2. AMDH leader, interview by the author, Oct. 5, 2016, Rabat.

in how to best resonate with the public. This variance of frames spurred by the king's concessions was the first major blow to the F20's survival.

The Moroccan regime's concerted policy of concessions followed by repression led to the F20's eventual demobilization. The F20 was initially united, but this harmony changed following the king's March 9 speech. The speech triggered internal conflicts about how the F20 would remain relevant and resonate with the public. These concessions also coincided with varied repression campaigns. Smear campaigns targeting the F20's most visible activists began in February 2011 and continued throughout the movement's activity. For example, charismatic activist Osama El-Khalifi became one of the most visible figureheads of the movement and was the target of various smear campaigns. The government-initiated smear campaign also took place online and portrayed F20 figureheads as atheists, "drinkers of alcohol, Christian converts," and sympathetic to the separatist Polisario Front (Desrues 2013, 418). Within the F20, this smear campaign led to conflicts, especially between Islamists and leftists.

In addition to offering concessions and engaging in smear campaigns, the regime also sought to prevent further mobilization through direct repression. Harsher nationwide repression that was aimed at dispersing or preventing protests began in May 2011 and intensified during the referendum period in July 2011 (Molina 2011, 441; Benchemsi 2014, 200). This repression campaign coincided with national media framing that the F20 had been hijacked by Islamist and leftist radicals (Molina 2011, 441). For instance, in May 2011, government spokesmen publicly warned that the F20 did not truly want reform but served the agenda of extreme leftists and Islamists.[3] This negative framing, in turn, led to internal conflicts about how to go forward as a social movement. These conflicts divided the social movement, which was also becoming increasingly alienated from the public. In other words, as more revolutionary demands began to permeate the F20, so did internal conflicts about diagnostic and prognostic frames. As we will see, the divide between "reformist monarchists" and

---

3. "Morocco Says Islamists, Leftists Stirring Protests," Reuters, May 23, 2011, https://in.reuters.com/article/idINIndia-57218720110523.

more "revolutionary republicans" became visible after the March 9 speech and continued to intensify and become more visible to the public leading up to the referendum campaign. Reformist monarchists want to maintain the monarchy and demanded reforms to the existing monarchical system. However, revolutionary republicans want a regime without a king and aspire to implement a democratic multiparty republic.

Concessions interact with internal factors, like how to frame the movement, to demonstrate how demobilization occurs. The combination of concessions, smear campaigns, and direct repression led to "framing crises" within the F20. Specifically, diagnostic and prognostic framing of the F20 was becoming a common source of contention within committee meetings, which manifested into a social movement with divergent messages and goals. This chapter builds on framing literature by using the case of the F20 to reveal how government concessions followed by repression and counterframing impacted the F20's internal movement dynamics.

More specifically, we will see that the king's concessionary March 9 speech categorically addressed the F20's main demands, which convinced many in the public and some activists that the F20's demands were sufficiently met. This depletion of the F20's initial grievances sparked internal disputes and a "framing crisis" within the movement. The F20, as I show, shifted from being a strictly reformist movement to a movement with mixed demands and frames, ranging from reformist to revolutionary. The lack of a unified frame and demands led to a movement that no longer connected with the Moroccan public. Moreover, direct and indirect repression was strategically implemented after unprecedented change through concessions was achieved. In essence, concessions in conjunction with repression helped demobilize the F20.

Movement Framing and Problem Depletion

Gamson (1975) believes movements start to decline when they overuse resources, while McAdam (2010) argues that dwindling political opportunities and incremental lack of support for a social movement lead to its decline. Davenport departs from these structuralist theories by analyzing movements themselves and finds that when movement demands are met (or appear to be met), then fractionalization and subsequent demobilization may occur: "A reduced sense of organizational support may provoke, exacerbate, or exist along with fractionalization and polarization in an SMO [social movement organization] as individuals attempt to address the threatening change in the environment, resulting in even greater dissention. In this context, it may become exhausting for participants to justify to themselves as well as others the reasonable nature of what they are doing, which results in demobilization" (2015, 40). I build on this finding and theorize that when there is public perception of problem depletion (initial demands are sufficiently being met), then social movements experiment with different frames to address and solve the perceived problem depletion. In cases where the leader has a credible history of declaring and implementing reforms, this stage of reorienting demands within heterogenous movements following problem depletion may often lead to fractionalization of the movement and a subsequent disunity in frames. If the public views reforms as a sufficient response to protests and trust that a leader will implement reforms, then internal framing disputes can occur, which focus on changing tactics and frames in order to attract public support again.[4]

Internal frame disputes are disputes around the diagnostic and prognostic frames (Benford 1993). Benford finds that frame disputes occur when differences within a movement arise about how to portray the movement in a way that maximizes mobilization (1993, 691). Similarly, I argue that framing disputes can lead to a framing crisis, where social movements try to change diagnostic frames (whom to blame) and prognostic frames (how to solve a problem), which subsequently leads to divergent motivational frames and messages.[5] In other words, there is no longer a united

---

4. According to the 2013 Arab Barometer, four-fifths of Moroccans opted for incremental change over change all at once, while more than half believe the government is undertaking far-reaching reforms. Moreover, most (56 percent) of Moroccans say they did not participate in "Arab Spring" protests because it was not important or they did not care to participate, and 80 percent believe that the 2011 constitution played an important role in ensuring separation of powers between the legislative and executive branches.

5. As indicated above, the conditions for this framing crisis to occur are that the social movement is heterogenous and the leader/regime in question has a history of declaring and implementing reforms.

frame. I build on the premise, like Davenport (2015), that movements try to ensure survival, even if many of the initial demands are met. For the F20, a framing crisis following the king's systematic concessions to demands led to fracturing when counterframing by the government occurred. As we will see, F20 members disagreed on how to convince a conservative and monarchically loyal public to support and join F20 protests. Moreover, preexisting ideological cleavages facilitated increased conflict, as Islamists and secular leftists disagreed on various issues, like the presence of religious symbols and slogans within protests. For instance, an Islamist F20 activist made it clear that differences in slogans were a contentious issue for the movement: "Ideologically speaking, the difference was clear at so many levels—namely, slogans."[6] Another prominent leftist and leader of an F20 support committee expressed how the movement's "colors" changed from a united movement to a movement where ideological divides became more evident: "The JCO would have their beards and Islamic dress, and the DWP would have pictures of Che Guevara, and the Amazigh activists [would have] their flags, and the Salafists [would have] their clothes and slogans. So, the colors of the movement began to change and there was no longer that one color which existed on February 20, 2011—which was the color of the youth. So, the movement began to decline."[7] Activists across all ideologies similarly sensed that these differences became more evident and defined within the movement after the king's March 9 speech.

Studying frames allows us to understand why, how, and when messages from social movements resonate (or not) with a public. Strategic framing processes are not limited to social movements. States and power holders, which have more material and cultural resources, often have an upper hand in constructing effective frames—especially when power holders are viewed as legitimate (Johnston and Noakes 2005, 105). Moreover, the "state and media control more cultural resources than your typical social movement" (17). Environmental structural changes, like the announcement and implementation of reforms, rise to power in certain political parties, and

6. Hizb al-Umma member, interview by the author, Nov. 15, 2016, Meknes.
7. Majlis Dahm leader, interview by the author, Feb. 21, 2017, Rabat.

the referendum campaign and early legislative elections also affect the relevance and compatibility of frames with the public. In essence, a secondary implication of this chapter for social movement studies is that changes in the political environment interact with social movement framing processes that can in turn ultimately lead to a movement's decline. Johnston and Noakes note that "when political structures change, adaptations in framing can open new opportunities for movement development" (2005, 23). Here I show the converse: how changes in environmental political structures can lead to movement demobilization and decline.

Benford and Snow (2000) find that collective-action frames can be schematized into diagnostic, prognostic, and motivational frames. All social movements need to diagnose a problem or set of grievances. Diagnostic framing moves beyond simply addressing a problem to framing problems in a way that resonates with people. For instance, framing LGBT rights as a human rights issue in the United States was an effective way to attract support beyond the LGBT community to others that are concerned with defending human rights in general (Holzhacker 2014). After diagnosing the problem, prognostic framing is the "articulation of a proposed solution to the problem, or at least a plan of attack, and the strategies for carrying out the plan" (Benford and Snow 2000, 616). Finally, motivational framing is how mobilization occurs. Motivational framing can attract or deter bystanders from joining a social movement depending on how the issue is framed. For instance, Benford (1993) finds that motivational vocabulary concerning severity, urgency, efficacy, and propriety emerged during the US disarmament movement. Put simply, diagnostic framing addresses what the problem is and where to attribute blame. Prognostic framing addresses what the demands of the movement should be and how to "solve the problem." Motivational framing concerns framing the movement in way to motivate people to join.

Benford and Snow call for more studies to research the relationship between "the conditions that affect the construction and adoption of various vocabularies of motive as well as assess their relative impact on social movement participation, collective identity processes, and other movement framing activities" (2000, 617–18). Said differently, we know that symbols and language need to resonate within the environment in which a social movement operates; however, how internal discussions around movement framing impact social movement participation and decline is understudied. Moreover, studies specifically addressing the relationship between achieving initial movement goals and social movement demobilization are limited. In the next section, I outline how concessions and repression affected internal dynamics within the F20 and facilitated the movement's demobilization.

The Reformist Movement

To understand when a regime's mixed policy of concessions and repression convinces activists to cease protesting, it is important to understand how the F20 came to be viewed as less reformist and more revolutionary in its demands. The F20 was able to unite previous enemies into a social movement that was initially reformist in nature. This cohesiveness is important for the F20, since ideologically based conflicts have a long history within Morocco, especially within universities, and many F20 activists were previous ideological enemies. Interviewees often reminded me that prior to the F20, Islamists were accused of killing leftist student activists and that members of the Amazigh cultural movement also had recurring conflicts with both Islamists and leftists.[8] Nevertheless, the abstract "injustice frames" in conjunction with the movement's reformist demands resonated with an array of F20 members, uniting them around reforming, rather than overthrowing, the Moroccan regime. According to an F20 cofounder: "This is the first time in the history of Morocco that parties and powers from far ends are united. This is the first experience in Morocco. We have not lived it before."[9] My fieldwork revealed that ideologically based conflicts eventually occurred within the F20 and that the F20's united reformist goals eventually changed. The increased visibility of the F20's more revolutionary activists helped further demobilize the movement by internally dividing groups within the movement, which led to a disunity in demands and frames.

8. DWP member from M'rirt, interview by the author, Oct. 13, 2016, Rabat.
9. F20 cofounder, interview by the author, Oct. 1, 2016, Rabat.

Table 2
The F20's United Frames, February–March 2011

The F20's diagnostic framing *What is the problem?* *Who do we blame?*	*Main problems*: monarchical absolutism, lack of democracy, corruption and electoral fraud, unemployment, police brutality, and equality for Amazigh people *Attribution of blame*: the Makhzen, Prime Minister Fassi, and local government leaders
The F20's prognostic framing *How to solve the problem?*	*Solutions to the problem*: reform the constitution, transition from monarchical absolutism to constitutional monarchy, end corruption, free and fair elections, and making Amazigh an official language *Secondary demands*: more economic opportunities, better education, and an improved health-care system
The F20's motivational framing *How do we frame the movement and motivate people to join?**	*Frames*: "Freedom, Dignity, and Social Justice," "The People Want to Change the Constitution," and "Down with Autocracy"

*These motivational frames tended to highlight the severity of regime corruption and lack of democracy, while also linking their causes to the events in Tunisia and Egypt in order to highlight the urgency to protest and "take advantage" of achieving goals during the protest wave engulfing the Arab world.

Initially, all groups within the F20's umbrella tended to agree on what the main problems were and who was to blame, which gave rise to the broad yet effective motivational slogans of the F20: "Freedom, Dignity, and Social Justice."[10] Table 2 presents the diagnostic, prognostic, and motivational frames of the F20 during the first two months of its activity.

It is not uncommon for social movements to have disagreements about prognostic frames and subsequently fracture (Haines 1996; Benford

10. "Injustice frames" allude to emotion to dramatize and blame power holders for a perceived injustice.

and Snow 2000). Movement members and organizations generally agree on the problem, but they may not agree on how to solve it. Therefore, the root of the problem here is deciding how to solve a problem (that is, what to demand). The F20 initially framed itself as a reformist movement solely asking for institutional changes; however, many F20 members admitted that the true goal of some members (for example, the JCO, the DWP, and some independent activists) within the movement was the overthrow of the regime. Since this outcome would not have been popular with the public and would have led to massive repression by the government, such revolutionaries (especially members of political parties) within the F20 would rarely openly call for ousting of the king during F20 committee meetings and protests. For example, the largest Islamist component of the F20, the JCO, openly rejected the monarchy and the king's position in power (Cavatorta 2007). As noted by Francesco Cavatorta (2007), the JCO rejected participating in institutions and negotiating with the monarchy, but at the same time refused to call for a revolution within the F20. Like other components within the F20, a possible explanation for why the JCO avoids an openly revolutionary frame is because it is unpopular with the Moroccan public. Indeed, more than 86 percent of the population thinks that political reforms should incrementally occur (Abdel-Samad 2014).

The F20 strategically framed itself in reformist terms in order to reso-nate with the Moroccan general public. A leader of the AMDH made this point clear when asked about the ideological stance of the movement: "The F20 was pragmatic. . . . Things would happen quickly, and there would not be time to have purposeful discussions about identity and whatnot. The discussions would concern 'what will we do,' 'what are our demands,' 'what is the future.'"[11] Strategic framing is common within social movements. As Benford and Snow demonstrate, framing processes are "deliberative, utilitarian, and goal directed," like gaining more recruits or mobilizing current members of the social movement (2000, 624). Therefore, move-ments are careful about the image they send to the public, and the F20 was especially strategic about the public role that Islamists played in the

11. AMDH leader, interview by the author, Oct. 5, 2016, Rabat.

movement. Initially, Islamists were simultaneously present and invisible within the F20. For example, some leftist interviewees felt that the presence of women in burqas would dissuade bystanders from joining F20 protests since it would be perceived as a movement that accepted Salafist principles. A Moroccan journalist who covered the movement indicated that the F20 was a movement with a leftist/progressive face but with an Islamic body. This point was clearly demonstrated by the agreement among both Islamists and leftists to limit the Islamist media presence: "The Islamists did not talk with the media. It was the Left and the cyber militants that did."[12] Moreover, as indicated by a JCO leader, "The JCO composed a big part of the movement, but we would not lead the marches in the beginning, and we did not have a say in the press."[13] Furthermore, in what would become a point of contention following the king's concessions, the JCO initially agreed to refrain from chanting Islamic slogans or raising religious banners during protests and marches.

There was a concerted effort within the F20 to have secular and moderate groups at the forefront of protests.[14] This strategy was meant to portray the F20 as secular and inclusive of all ideologies and Moroccan society. Elaborating on why the JCO voluntarily agreed to stay out of the media and lead protests and marches, a JCO leader and F20 activist claimed, "We did all of this to preserve the movement and its power to guarantee the ideological diversity of F20. . . . We did not try to portray the movement with a specific identity. We believed that this movement was for all people."[15] Another effect of this secular framing was that the F20 decided to hold weekly protests every Sunday and not following prayers on Friday, as is typical throughout the MENA region. Moreover, slogans and banners were strictly secular, with no Islamic references. Leftist interviewees admitted that they tended to control which slogans and

12. Journalist/activist, interview by the author, Jan. 12, 2017, Casablanca.

13. Ex-political prisoner and F20 activist from Rif region, interview by the author, Oct. 4, 2016, Rabat.

14. By moderate, I mean not challenging the monarchical system and calling for reforms.

15. JCO leader, interview by the author, Oct. 31, 2016, Rabat.

banners would be used in protests, despite the JCO's power in numbers: "In terms of size, it was clear that the Islamists were powerful, and their withdrawal in December 2012 was felt. . . . But in terms of slogans, we were smart and agreed on the slogans. Most slogans were about freedom and democracy."[16] Islamists, however, began to experiment in increasing their visibility (leading protests and speaking with the media) and in using Islamist slogans and banners in March 2011. Reports noted that Islamists dominated protests in Casablanca on March 6, 2011, but not in other cities.[17] As we will see in the next section, beginning in March 2011, there was variance in collective-action frames regarding how Islamic and more revolutionary frames would resonate with the public.

Demobilizing the Movement with Concessions

Although problem depletion should seemingly satisfy a movement and lead to its demise, this outcome is not always the case. When the king responded to the F20's demands with reforms, the F20 needed to convince the public that there was still good reason to support the movement. After all, the F20 overwhelmingly rejected the reforms—it ultimately boycotted the July referendum—and planned major marches and protests in response to the proposed reforms. However, the king's series of concessions convinced many within the public, and even some F20 members, to no longer support the movement. A journalist who covered the F20 protests in Casablanca made it clear that the general public's perception of the F20 changed after the king's concessionary speech: "People believed in the king's plan [March 9 reforms] and no longer in the F20's plan. So, they [the general public] stopped believing in the movement after the reforms; they viewed it as repetitious." The same journalist also emphasized that although the F20 rejected the March 9 speech, they also did not know "how to respond to the reforms."[18] Another journalist, who was fired from his position because of his activity with the F20, expressed a similar

---

16. F20 independent leftist, interview by the author, Sept. 19, 2016, Rabat.

17. Maghress, http://www.maghress.com/hibapress/24497.

18. Journalist participant observer, interview by the author, Sept. 26, 2016, Casablanca.

sentiment about what the average Moroccan felt about reforms: "The average people saw the reforms. . . . They saw that many demands were met with the constitution."[19] This situation begs the question of what happens to a heterogeneous social movement when their main demands are seemingly granted by those individuals in power?

In the view of many F20 activists, reforms (like repression) hurt the movement. Indeed, activists I spoke with often refer to the king's reforms as *darabat*—literally "blows" in Arabic. In the words of one activist, "The regime decided to use a nonviolent policy that led to the failure of the F20 movement."[20] If we view concessions and reforms as potential threats to a movement's survival, then viewing concessions as problem depletion is indeed a blow in the view of a social movement. Among F20 activists, concessions that aimed at systematically satisfying certain groups within the F20 were clearly viewed as threats:

> The carrot was to buy off the unions by giving the public workers a pay increase. Also, they found work for young unemployed graduates— almost four thousand. This never happened before. Until today they still pay them. . . . He [the king] did these things to calm the streets a little. He also freed many political prisoners, like our general secretary [of Hizb al-Umma] along with some Salafist leaders, in order to alleviate the tension in the street. We also wanted a democratic constitution, so he formed a committee to make a constitution. They [the members of this committee] were picked by the king, and they came up with the 2011 constitution, which was a complete failure. It did not respond to any of our demands.[21]

To be clear, reforms did not affect the movement directly, but rather influenced "how the public saw the F20 movement."[22] Therefore, the reforms affected internal discussions about the strategy and tactics the F20 would

19. F20 activist and journalist, interview by the author, Jan. 19, 2017, Rabat.

20. Hizb al-Umma member, interview by the author, Nov. 15, 2016, Meknes.

21. Hizb al-Umma and UMT labor leader, interview by the author, Feb. 26, 2017, Tangier.

22. Independent activist, interview by the author, Sept. 22, 2016, Mohammedia.

take postreforms. Another F20 activist from the rural town of M'rirt emphasizes that the rejection of the reforms occurred "directly after the speech" and that the first point of contention was the fact that the committee formed to change the constitution was appointed by the king. The same activist notes that activists in the town were directed by local authorities to cease all street protests and that the handful of activists who did decide to demonstrate against the reforms were "each escorted by four policemen, and they took us from the square and to the CDT headquarters so that we were not harmed."[23] In other words, we see that initially the regime was hesitant to directly repress demonstrators, as doing so would likely have veered attention away from the king's unprecedented reforms. An AMDH leader argues that the presentation of the constitutional reforms deceitfully convinced people that major changes were being undertaken:

> There are various reasons [that protests lessened], the power of the state, I mean how the constitution of 2011 was presented. Even the educated people in the beginning were tricked and said that "this is a huge reform and there was never a constitution like it, and we did not expect all of this." However, the constitution had everything and nothing. It had nice general answers, but in content it does not answer the demands of human rights and law because the king still rules all; all the powers remain in his hand.[24]

The March 9 speech surprised many with the reforms announced, but during the speech the king mentioned previously implemented reforms, like the creation of the Justice and Reconciliation Commission along with advancements made in women's rights.[25] The signal to the public was clear: the F20's main grievances would be addressed through reforms, and the king asserted that this promise was legitimate by referencing his previous reforms.

23. Al-Naj leader, interview by the author, Oct. 13, 2016, Meknes.

24. AMDH leader, interview by the author, Oct. 16, 2017, Rabat.

25. The Équité et Réconciliation was a royal decree to investigate arrests, abuses, and disappearances during the reign of King Hassan II. Advancements in women's rights were gained through the reform of the Family Code Law.

The king categorically responded to the F20's demands through the March 9 speech. Reforming the constitution, establishing measures to end corruption, recognizing the Amazigh language, and devolving some of the king's powers were all core demands by the F20, which the king addressed. In the speech, the king declared that he would form a committee to change the constitution,[26] establish more oversight and accountability of public office holders, and propose an independent judicial branch.[27] Given that the king has historically implemented the reforms that he has announced, the general public had good reason to believe that the March 9 speech would lead to a similar outcome of implementation. F20 members, however, overwhelmingly viewed things differently, and more revolutionary elements began to "show their teeth" following the king's concessions. The movement increasingly adopted a more revolutionary frame that went beyond the initial, strictly reformist, frame. Mekouar states that there was an "early moderate character" of the F20 that "increased the base of incoming supporters" (2016, 97). Still, groups that were viewed as extreme and that did not accept working for change through existing institutions, like the JCO and the DWP, became more dominant and visible after the March 9 speech. Their new prognostic frame was a rejection of the monarchy without a clear path for the future. Activists from more moderate (reformist) parties, like the USFP, became increasingly concerned with the visibility and perceived dominance of more revolutionary elements of the F20. For instance, a USFP leader in Casablanca noted that overthrowing the king always "existed in the hearts" of some activists, but became more visible after the March 9 speech, which "devastated the movement."[28] The presence of these revolutionaries and the JCO, and how they tried to frame the movement, became even more visible following state repression that followed the March 9 reforms.

26. The Advisory Committee for Constitutional Reform is colloquially known as the Mounini Committee.

27. The F20 had an array of demands. Some secondary demands include more economic opportunities, better education, and an improved health-care system.

28. USFP leader, interview by the author, Nov. 26, 2016, Casablanca.

As framing conflicts among reformists and revolutionaries ensued, the regime decided to selectively use direct repression. This selective repression tended to target Islamists and was followed by the concessionary March 9 speech. Protests on March 13, 2011, rejecting the king's proposed reforms were violently dispersed by police. The police actions resulted in fractures, broken ribs, and concussions. The JCO suffered most of the repression on March 13, which led the group to issue a statement condemning the "cosmetic" reforms and the state of human rights in Morocco.[29] Why the JCO in particular was the target is not clear, but activists confirmed media reports that following the March 9 speech, repression tended to target the JCO. Some activists claimed that targeting the JCO was a strategy by the regime to divide the movement. Others claimed that the JCO suffered so much repression during this time since they simply outnumbered any other organization within the F20. A JCO general leader claimed that repression increased after the March 9 speech mainly because there was an expectation by the regime that protests would cease after the reforms: "The state thought that after the king's speech, protests would stop or weaken and recede, but the opposite occurred. The marches that occurred in April and May were the strongest marches."[30] Regardless of the reasons the JCO suffered massive repression on March 13, 2011, the increased "price paid" by the JCO led them to more openly "speak their minds." The enhanced visibility of JCO members, in turn, resulted in the perception of increasing Islamist domination of the F20 that forced many to either not join or leave F20 protests.[31] Similarly, on March 20, 2011, a massive march by the F20 was organized throughout the country, again in response to the March 9 speech; however, the protests were for the most part peaceful.

The restraint on behalf of the regime may be owing to the international attention Morocco received following March 13, 2011. Amnesty

---

29. "Youth of Justice and Charity: We Bear the Consequences of the Makhzani Repression of the Ruling Regime," Maghress, Mar. 15, 2011, https://www.maghress.com /sawtalhoriya/210.

30. JCO leader, interview by the author, Oct. 31, 2016, Rabat.

31. Independent leftist, interview by the author, Sept. 19, 2016, Casablanca.

International, for instance, urged Morocco to change its repressive tactics and expressed that Moroccans must be free to protest: "The unnecessary acts of violence witnessed last weekend are a disturbing regression and make a mockery of the Moroccan King's promise a few days earlier to undertake fundamental reform and uphold human rights" (Amnesty International USA 2011). Despite government restraint, the tone of some of the F20's demands became more revolutionary across the nation. On March 20, 2011, the main chant in Rabat, for example, was "The people want to overthrow tyranny."[32] In Guelmim, a small city in southern Morocco, F20 protests split, with one group attempting to storm local state headquarters and clashing with security forces, while another group stayed in public areas and remained peaceful.[33] In Agadir and Casablanca, some protesters commemorated past human rights abuses by the state: "After the repression, the movement wanted to commemorate the martyrs from the 1981 Bread Uprising.[34] In Casablanca they made a staged graveyard. . . . Moroccans understood that they must demand for rights, and this still exists today."[35]

Vilifying the F20

I met Reda, an F20 cofounder and outspoken critic of the regime, early in the morning at an empty café in the heart of Casablanca. Reda's reaction to my questions was always animated and, at times, visibly resentful. After Reda's orange juice arrived, we began talking about the repression against the F20. He became especially upset when talking about state repression and would incessantly tap his bottle of juice with his finger

32. "Tens of Thousands in the Rallies of Rabat, Al-Bayda, Fez and Others This Morning," Maghress, Mar. 20, 2011, https://www.maghress.com/arrifinu/38457.

33. "Report on the Protests in Guelmim on February 20," Maghress, Feb. 21, 2011, https://www.maghress.com/wadnon/1790.

34. The 1981 Bread Rising in Casablanca (Black Saturday) refers to the massacre of hundreds of demonstrators by the Moroccan regime against activists protesting rising food prices.

35. "Radical Communist" F20 member, interview by the author, Dec. 12, 2016, Agadir.

when discussing this topic. He emphasized that although direct repression occurred against the movement, it was the smear campaign that left him unemployed and outcast. Tapping away at his bottle of juice, Reda made it clear that he resented the media reports defaming him. Reda mentioned that his life had been threatened and that he had faced direct repression by security forces; however, it was the smear campaign against him that made him tap his finger on his drink. Reda directly faulted the state for his unemployment. The uncomfortable interview concluded by Reda saying that there would be a "round two" of demonstrations in the future. Weeks later, protests erupted in the northern coastal city of Al-Hoceima. I offered to pay for our drinks and was surprised that Reda did not try to pay—a custom in Morocco.

Following the March 9 speech, proregime websites along with public media outlets intensified the smear campaign that started in February 2011. These campaigns targeted specific individuals, like Reda. Owing to familial and community pressure following such smear campaigns, the campaigns had especially devastating effects on women figureheads, who often left the movement as a result.[36] An F20 cofounder was attacked online after sources revealed that he was living with his girlfriend, a punishable offense in Morocco. The same activist was accused of not being born in Morocco.[37] Other online videos would link leftists to Sahrawi separatists and would often portray them as Algerian operatives and as not compatible with Moroccan culture. An AMDH leader elaborated on the smear campaign against activists in Morocco: "We call them new forms of repression in Morocco. . . . They are webpages that use known journalists—in order to have credibility—but specialize in stopping activism. They write false reports, whether in magazines or Facebook, and specialize in propaganda against activists."[38] In general, there was a consensus among interviewees that the smear campaigns played an especially big role in weakening support for the movement by convincing the public that it was not in line

36. AMDH leader, interview by the author, Oct. 5, 2016, Rabat.
37. F20 cofounder, interview by the author, Oct. 6, 2016, Casablanca.
38. AMDH leader, interview by the author, Oct. 5, 2016, Rabat.

with Moroccan culture and norms.[39] This smear campaign was especially problematic for some members of the pro-individual-liberties organization MALI.[40] For example, a self-proclaimed universalist-feminist leader of MALI[41] found it difficult to have slogans for gender equality, personal liberties, or freedom of religion within F20 protests, because the slogans would not resonate with Moroccan cultural norms.[42] The same cofounder indicated how "moderates" and not Islamists within the F20 were conscious about how the public would perceive them.[43] In one case, the MALI cofounder was confronted by leftists about how smoking (as a woman) within protests would hurt the movement's image: "In Morocco it is complicated for women to smoke. You have women like me that say: 'Fuck! I am a woman, and I smoke!' and we had a lot of activists that did not want women smoking during the demonstrations, because Moroccan society says we have to hide it because we are women—so that Moroccan people will like the movement and support it."[44] As we see, even leftist activists (who often demand gender equality) were careful to frame the movement in a way that did not contradict Moroccan norms and culture. F20 members attempted to make the movement compatible with average Moroccans to mobilize supporters, which is why activists did not want women to smoke during demonstrations. Counterframing of the F20 initially took aim at F20 figureheads and members of MALI and the JCO. These smear campaigns portrayed the movement either as dominated by Islamist fundamentalists or as Western inspired and anti-Islamic. The contradiction between simultaneously attacking Islamists for being religious extremists and secular liberals for not accepting Islamic norms is obvious, but the smear campaign was effective in that it did heighten internal discussions

39. JCO leader, interview by the author, Oct. 31, 2016, Rabat.

40. According to the MALI, personal liberties include LGBT rights, freedom of religion (having a choice to believe in any or no region), and gender equality.

41. Universalism implies human rights should be the same everywhere, regardless of the context. In other words, universalists do not believe in cultural or religious relativism.

42. MALI cofounder, interview by the author, May 7, 2017, Rabat.

43. This specific interviewee's use of the word *moderate* refers to liberals and leftists.

44. MALI cofounder, interview by the author, May 7, 2017, Rabat.

about the strategic visibility of "extremist" groups within the F20: "The penetration by the regime of the movement led to marginalized issues making their way inside the movement. We don't have any problems with homosexuals or anyone. These are other issues. Moroccans are contradictory—some pray, some drink, and some drink before praying. To make the movement fail, these issues started to become important—like homosexuality. Therefore, the union among leftists and Islamists weakened."[45] A leftist cofounder also agreed that discussing culturally sensitive topics was a "trap" that the movement should have avoided: "If you exclusively talk about individual freedoms, you're empowering the authoritarians in Morocco because you automatically turn against society and not against the regime."[46] With exception to some independent activists and MALI members, most interviewees agree that explicitly demanding LGBT rights is not feasible in Morocco, and therefore personal freedoms were seen as a subset under the broad frame of freedom.

An independent F20 activist who coordinated the Media Committee of the F20 opposed the activists who would not tackle "sensitive issues." In his words, "The identity of the F20 is one of modernity, so we can't say that we are for freedom and reject personal freedoms. I don't understand an Islamist who participates with the F20 clearly calling for freedoms and justice while being against sexual freedom or freedom of religion. So, we wanted to discuss these topics with them. . . . These discussions . . . these philosophical discussions, created a lot of conflicts within the movement."[47] Therefore, some activists attempted to discuss sexual freedoms, freedom of religion, and LGBT rights, but the movement tended to relegate these issues, if not ignore them altogether. Again, this reaction was not always a political decision, but a strategic one. An independent F20 activist who is publicly atheist and advocates openly for freedom of faith mentioned that even members from MALI "delayed their politics," since the movement initially "wanted the amalgamation of the biggest

45. Two Hizb al-Umma members, interview by the author, Nov. 5, 2016, Rabat.
46. F20 cofounder, interview by the author, Oct. 6, 2016, Rabat.
47. Independent activist, interview by the author, Sept. 21, 2016, Mohammedia.

number of people possible, so we couldn't fight with the JCO or the Salaf-ists and call for these demands."[48]

The F20's broadly construed justice frame of "Freedom, Dignity, and Social Justice" encompasses culturally sensitive issues like gender equal-ity and LGBT rights, without specifically mentioning them. In the words of one Islamist participant: "Since the first slogan includes 'social justice,' this means that the issue of inheritance would be solved, so you don't need to use those titles [referring to gender equality] to create conflict."[49] The strategic exclusion of certain frames is what Lavine, Cobb, and Rous-sin (2017) refer to as label-frame contraction. In the case of the F20, the group not only sought to excise frames concerning gender equality and LGBT rights, but also attempted to exclude revolutionary frames that went beyond the initial reformist demands of the movement. Some leftist mem-bers of the F20 not only feared internal divisions that resulted from the regime's counterframing, but also feared that the mere presence of the JCO within the F20 posed a threat to the movement. In their view, the F20 would no longer resonate with a public that was increasingly fearful of sectarian rife. The fear on behalf of some F20 activists was that continuing protests would ultimately empower Islamist extremists.[50]

Therefore, many leftist activists felt a need to address the identity of the F20 and, more important, the presence of the JCO within the move-ment. After March 2011, the F20 also started discussing issues related to the identity of the movement, and these discussions initiated ideologically based conflicts: "We never spoke about the identity [of the F20]. Therefore, after . . . we started to say, okay—who are we? We started these workshops of values; what values do we believe in? Here also the problems started."[51]

48. Independent F20 activist, interview by the author, Feb. 22, 2017, Rabat.

49. Two Hizb al-Umma members, interview by the author, Nov. 5, 2016, Rabat. (The interviewee is referring to the demands by some F20 members that women have equal rights to land inheritance, which Islamists and many conservatives in Morocco are staunchly against.)

50. JCO leader, interview by the author, Oct. 31, 2016, Rabat.

51. F20 independent activist, interview by the author, Sept. 22, 2016, Rabat.

The F20 figureheads realized that Islamic framing of the movement would not resonate with all Moroccans.[52] Thus, F20 members agreed to ban religious slogans, and the eventual increase in Islamic slogans became contentious.

> In the beginning, the agreement [with the JCO] was no religious slogans—"No Allah Akbar" or anything. And they followed this, but they abided by it until they became more dominant in the committees and contributed in the demonstrations. . . . I will give you an example, in the first three days of the F20, [the JCO] did not stop protesting because of the Adnan [Islamic call to prayer]. When they heard the Adnan, some of them would pray here on the side, like three to four would get together and pray. After a while, they tried to have demonstrations begin before or after the Adnan. We then started hearing religious slogans like "There is no God, but God," etc. So, this scared people. A big part of the citizens came to see us but did not become involved [in protests]. . . . The JCO's slogans would scare people, and this was the beginning of the weakening of the F20.[53]

Concerns about the large Islamist presence within the F20 were repeatedly mentioned by leftist interviewees, especially in relation to how the public would perceive the F20 if Islamists were "too" visible. For example, one F20 independent activist mentioned how inhabitants from Rabat, specifically, were not accustomed to a large Islamist presence on the streets: "The people in Rabat were not used to this sight. You might see them in the North or South [Salafists especially tend to be less popular in central Rabat], but not in Rabat. So, when they all came to Rabat, the people were scared. They were not used to this sight."[54] Islamist interviewees saw things differently. In their view, Morocco, an Islamic and Arab society, would naturally be attracted to such slogans. In one instance, Islamists and leftists directly

52. The committee is known as the National Support Council for Support of the F20.
53. Majlis Dahm leader, interview by the author, Feb. 21, 2017, Rabat.
54. Ex-journalist and F20 independent, interview by the author, Jan. 19, 2017, Rabat.

confronted each other during demonstrations after Islamic slogans were chanted in solidarity with Syrian activists: "We [Islamists] were surprised to hear calls for gender equality. . . . Often, we would march together in large protests, and suddenly conflicts would erupt between JCO members and leftists concerning Islamic slogans for the Syrians."[55]

According to Islamists from the JCO and Hizb al-Umma, framing the movement in religious terms would culturally resonate with the public. Nevertheless, the JCO did not become more visible until after the king's March 9 speech and especially during and after one of the F20's biggest marches on April 24, 2011, when, according to state estimates, twenty-seven thousand people protested throughout the country.[56] Following the April 2011 march, there was a perception among leftist members that the media started to focus on the presence of Islamists in the F20, and the JCO "stole the show."[57] Moreover, during the April 24 protest, a large Salafist-Islamist presence was reported for the first time, especially within Rabat's lower-income neighborhoods.[58] In essence, many leftists felt that there was a shift from framing the movement as secular and inclusive for all Moroccans. More important, they felt that this increased "religious framing" would be detrimental to the movement and not attract bystanders to support the F20.

Conclusion

For a frame to resonate with the public, congruence between societal belief systems and frames is necessary. Following the March 9 speech and the targeted repression against F20 figureheads and Islamists, discussions about the visibility and mere presence of Islamists in the F20 persisted. Discussions about what type of movement the F20 is and how it can respond to the consistent mix of concessions by the regime also weakened

---

55. Hizb al-Umma member, interview by the author, Nov. 5, 2016, Rabat.

56. "Marches in Several Cities of Morocco to Demand Political, Economic and Social Reforms," Maghress, Apr. 24, 2011, https://www.maghress.com/fr/mapfr/24351.

57. Independent F20 activist, interview by the author, Sept. 16, 2016, Casablanca.

58. "The April 24 March Roams the Popular Neighborhoods of Rabat," Hespress, Apr. 25, 2011, https://www.maghress.com/hespress/30790.

the F20. Concessions caused problem depletion and internal disputes and changed the initial political opportunities that the 2011 MENA Uprisings provided the F20.

As we will see in the next chapter, a new round of concession followed by repression demobilized the movement. The F20's internal conflicts intensified with a referendum campaign for a new constitution and direct repression against the movement. The king's concessions essentially convinced Moroccans that a movement was no longer needed. Repression followed each concession, which ultimately divided the movement. Some activists continued to push for reforms, while others called for revolution. The increasingly visible revolutionary elements within the movement convinced many Moroccans that the F20 no longer represented their interests. This chapter and the next demonstrate how strategically implemented concessions and repression demobilized the F20.

3

Repression

Crossing "Red Lines"

> I personally called for the overthrow of the regime within the F20,
> but today I would say no [to revolution]. If we actually overthrew the
> regime and took up arms, then our situation would be like Libya's
> today. . . . Morocco has a foundation, it's not great, but if there were
> violent protests, then we would have demolished this foundation.
> —F20 activist in Agadir

The civil wars in Libya and Syria served as an opportunity for the regime
to convince the general public of the danger that continued street protests
would cause. The images of conflict in both contexts made Moroccans
especially fearful of sectarianism and the potential rise of Islamists into
power, and the Moroccan regime took advantage of this situation. When
the king gave his March 9 speech, Libya was in the midst of a civil war
and mass protests were under way in Syria. Within a year Syria was in a
full-fledged civil war. The internal conflicts between Islamists and leftists within the F20 were amplified by the regional rise of sectarianism.
The increased visibility and religious framing within the F20 made some
within the general public fearful of continuing protests, and the regime
took advantage of this apprehension.

The violence from the civil wars engulfing Syria and Libya instigated
fear among activists that a continuation in protests may lead to violent
conflict. These regional events affected internal discussions within the F20
and how the public perceived the movement. As we will see, F20 activists increasingly became divided about whether the movement should
risk instability by increasing protests in new, densely populated, spaces

of major cities. Activists against increasing pressure on the regime were greatly affected by the scenes of violence pouring in from Yemen and eventually Syria. In the words of a current member of parliament who participated in the F20 movement: "What occurred in Syria and Libya had a huge effect on the movement. Al-Jazeera played a big role. People would say I don't have all of my rights, but at least I live with security and I can eat and drink."[1] Said differently, the violence from the civil wars in Syria and Libya forced many to fear that a continuation in protest activity might lead to the violence transmitted on TV and computer screens throughout Morocco.

Activists across ideologies informed me that the regime took advantage of the regional violence by contrasting Morocco's stability and reformist stances to the violent approaches taken by leaders in Syria and Libya.[2] In the words of one Democratic Way Party activist, "This was propagated by the state. That 'we are stable' and that 'we should not go down that path.' People got scared that things would get violent and that things would go down the path of Syria, Libya, and Yemen."[3] This sentiment even convinced F20 activists that "it would be better to take what we have [reforms] and see how things work out."[4] Islamist interviewees often felt that regional events had an especially big effect on how leftists treated them within the F20. For example, a JCO leader directly linked electoral victories by Islamists in Tunisia and Egypt to ideologically based conflicts within the F20: "The elections in Tunisia and Egypt paved the way for Islamist parties. So, leftists became afraid of participation in a protest movement that they would not benefit from. So, they [leftists] started to raise questions that led to conflict, and they insisted on giving a sense of a 'leftist identity' to the movement by demonizing some Islamist groups and their banners. Discussions began in the general assemblies that would prepare the marches." Another F20 independent activist felt that regional

1. CDT MP, interview by the author, Jan. 13, 2017, Rabat.
2. According to the 2016 Arab Barometer, Moroccans are most satisfied with the government's ability to provide security (90 percent), followed by narrowing the gap between rich and poor (58 percent).
3. DWP activist, interview by the author, Oct. 5, 2016, Rabat.
4. AMDH leader, interview by the author, Dec. 5, 2016, Rabat.

conflicts had an especially big effect on the middle class, which decided to vote over protest, in large part owing to their fear that Morocco could digress into violence:

> I think the biggest blow to the movement was the fear that pervaded Moroccans after what they saw in the Syrian and Yemeni scenarios. Some Moroccans started to say that "At least we achieved a new constitution and elections where a new party won first place and we have some sort of freedoms, so we should preserve what we accomplished and continue." So, lawyers, engineers, doctors, and teachers started going to the ballot boxes, and they voted for the PJD, even though they do not agree with the opinion of the party—even though they have bottles of wine at the dinner table—but they had confidence in the PJD's honesty and that [their electoral victory] would lead to stability. Stability for this class within society is important since they have houses and cars with bank loans, a child studying abroad that takes a trip to Spain or France once a year.[5]

An Amazigh activist had a similar analysis of the situation and linked the F20's demobilization to regional violence: "If Syria's and Libya's paths were different, then maybe the F20 would have continued, because the path over there affected Morocco's path too." Some activists believe that the Moroccan regime became more repressive following violence in Syria and Libya: "In the beginning, everything was peaceful, and the regime was peaceful too. But when things happened in Libya and Syria, the regime started to become more violent. When they became violent and the F20 movement saw what was happening in other countries, there was a type of fear among leaders."[6] It is clear that regional events did have a big effect on internal social movement dynamics in Morocco and perhaps even pushed the regime toward direct repression of the movement.

In May 2011, the government took on a harsher and more universal approach and repressed all F20 protests—no longer just targeting

5. F20 independent, interview by the author, Nov. 23, 2016, Rabat.
6. Amazigh movement leader, interview by the author, Dec. 8, 2016, Tangier.

Islamists in select cities. Specifically, violent nationwide repression began to intensify in mid-May as massive protests throughout the country persisted (Benchemsi 2014). Direct repression within Morocco usually involved security forces brutally beating protesters with batons during demonstrations. Security forces also raided, for the first time, the USP's main headquarters in Casablanca and beat various activists.[7] In the city of Safi, on Morocco's Atlantic Coast, a thirty-year-old protester succumbed to his wounds following harsh police repression.[8] Finally, the regime selectively arrested figureheads, often from the JCO or the extreme left (DWP), during protests—some of whom received death threats (Mekouar 2016). However, the most widespread use of direct repression occurred when F20 protests moved into Morocco's densely populated low-income neighborhoods, what Moroccans refer to as popular neighborhoods—referred to as al'ahya' al-shaebia in Arabic. These areas were not initially drawn to protests by the F20.

Moving Protests to the Neighborhoods: Between Anomic Threat and Opportunity

> There was repression for a reason. We went to the popular neighborhoods, and our discussions were not with the political elite, but with the people.
> —JCO member in Casablanca

Since the 2011 MENA Uprisings and the subsequent Occupy Wall Street movement in 2011, there has been increased attention paid to how protests interact with space (Sotiropoulos 2017). According to activists, where protests occurred in Morocco is especially important. Rather than confined to a square or large avenue, protests in the popular neighborhoods tended to take the form of marches that stretched for miles and gathered momentum as they progressed through the neighborhood's tight spaces. According to many F20 activists, these marches proved much more difficult for police to disperse. Wang Xu, Yu Ye, and Chan's study of space and

7. Majlis Dahm leader, interview by the author, Feb. 21, 2017, Rabat.
8. "Morocco's Uprisings and All the King's Men," Al-Jazeera English, June 5, 2011, https://www.aljazeera.com/features/2011/6/5/moroccos-uprisings-and-all-the-kings-men.

the Occupy Central Movement in Hong Kong finds that "spatial proximity helps strengthen social networks and makes it easier to assemble people" (2014, 2). In their case study, spatial proximity on college campuses facilitated mobilization, since homogenous networks of students encouraged each other to partake in protests. My interviews revealed a similar dynamic within communities that live within Morocco's popular neighborhoods.

Zartman (1988) coined the term *anomic threat* when outlining how Moroccan labor-union strikes in the 1980s attracted bystanders and grew into uncontrolled riots. Buehler makes the case that a similar "anomic threat" occurred during the union strikes of 2010 and early 2011. In the union strikes of both the 1980s and 2010–11, there is a mutual fear by both the regime and the unions that strikes "might escalate to similar forms of sporadic, uncontrollable urban instability" (2018, 150). A similar mutual fear by the regime and reformists within the F20 existed in 2011. Reformist F20 members repeatedly expressed their concerns that bringing protests to popular neighborhoods would lead Morocco to instability and chaos—similar to the chaos engulfing Libya and Syria at the time. Revolutionary F20 members, however, wanted to increase pressure on the regime. Revolutionaries believed that bringing demonstrations into these neighborhoods would successfully mobilize more Moroccans and subsequently better position the F20 to demand more fundamental changes—an "anomic opportunity." Some F20 activists wanted revolutionary change that necessitated mobilizing the lower-class masses in these neighborhoods. Reformists within the F20 recognized and feared the instability and looming repression that entering these neighborhoods would cause. Indeed, the regime's response to demonstrations in these neighborhoods was markedly harsh. Interviewees expressed that a rationale for the increased repression could be owing to the fact that the more extreme elements of the F20 were becoming increasingly visible and because the F20 was protesting more and more in popular neighborhoods.[9] This situation, according to activists, was dangerous for the regime, since the F20 mainly

---

9. The Al-Qaeda-linked terror attack on a Marrakech café frequented by tourists on April 28, 2011, was another possible reason repression increased in May.

mobilized the middle class, while the densely populated and lower-income areas (popular neighborhoods) were not initially drawn to protests. An F20 independent from Casablanca elaborates on why keeping the F20 out of these neighborhoods was so important to the regime: "It is the territory of INDH [National Initiative for Human Development],[10] which the state uses for its clientelism. They are also neighborhoods that have many Salafists, Islamists, and even [Islamist] radicals. So, in these neighborhoods, the Islamists are there, but the Left is not present in general."[11] Therefore, the F20's presence in these neighborhoods threatened the regime in two ways. First, it could lead base supporters and voters of loyalist parties to side with the F20. Second, it threatened mobilizing Islamists (often antiregime Salafists) in mass numbers. The same interviewee shed light on how a protest within an impoverished popular neighborhood of Casablanca, Sidi-Moumen, infamous for its poverty and support for Islamists, surprised and perhaps changed the perception of the F20: "The people in the neighborhood said, 'This is the first time that you come to our neighborhood'—it was interesting—the reception of the people in the poor neighborhoods where we would organize marches. Sometimes, we would have marches and some kids would say, 'When are you guys coming back?' [laughs]."[12] During the same time that the F20 was experimenting with entering popular neighborhoods, slogans during F20 marches continued taking an increasingly more revolutionary frame. During nationwide protests on May 22, 2011, slogans in Rabat included "Makhzen get out. Down with despotism," and protests started in the lower-income popular neighborhood of Akkari—the first time this had occurred. Reuters also reported that on May 22, 2011, some protesters were "becoming more outspoken about criticizing King Mohammed."[13]

10. The INDH is a World Bank–funded programs to improve living conditions of low-income areas in Morocco.

11. F20 independent, interview by the author, Oct. 26, 2017, Casablanca.

12. F20 independent, interview by the author, Oct. 26, 2016, Casablanca.

13. "Many Wounded as Moroccan Police Beat Protestors," Reuters, May 22, 2011, https://www.reuters.com/article/us-morocco-protests/dozens-wounded-as-moroccan-police-beat-protestors-idUSTRE74L2YK20110522.

During May 2011, the F20 decided to hold protests in popular neighborhoods of Rabat, Casablanca, Marrakech, and Tangier. The regime responded with harsh and violent repression throughout the country during the May 22 protests when the F20 held (or attempted to hold) protests in these popular neighborhoods. In Rabat, for instance, protests of all types usually occur in front of the parliament building or the Bab-al-Had Square. In Tangier, Fez, Tetouan, Agadir, Rabat, and Casablanca, the regime tried to curb the mass protests by blocking off alleys and small main squares within the popular neighborhoods. In some instances, the local police along with the national security forces also beat and dispersed protesters.[14] In Sebta, a popular neighborhood of Casablanca, videos reveal that security forces surrounded bleeding demonstrators, one of whom is unconscious and bleeding from the head.[15] In Mohammedia, a port city neighboring Casablanca, water cannons were used to disperse protesters, while five buses full of security forces came to the medium-size city in an attempt to prevent protests.[16] Foreign news sources widely reported the new wave of repression. France 24 characterized the repression as brutal and reported that protesters were violently beaten in alleys where the media was not allowed to film.[17]

On May 29, 2011, dozens were injured in an F20 march by security forces, and one protester was killed (Boukhars and Hamid 2011). During that same week, the minister of communication and leaders in the police force continued to publicly discredit the F20 by declaring that the movement had been taken over by Islamists and the Far Left.[18] The Moroccan

14. "Security Thwarts 'Insistence on Change' Rallies," *Hespress*, May 22, 2011, https://www.maghress.com/hespress/31925.

15. "There Is Blood in the Streets of Casablanca," YouTube, accessed Apr. 16, 2017, https://www.youtube.com/watch?time_continue=43&v=Z6pe5sOZsJk.

16. "The Authorities Resort to Force to Prevent the 'Insistence on Change' Rallies in the Cities of Rabat, Tangier, Mohammedia and Casablanca," Maghress, May 22, 2011, https://www.maghress.com/lakome/4959.

17. "Une manifestation à Casablanca réprimée avec une extrême brutalité," France 24, last modified May 31, 2011, https://observers.france24.com/fr/20110530-manifestants-casablanca-brutalite-policiers-repression-maroc.

18. "The February 20 Movement Was Swallowed Up by Islamists and Leftist Movements," Maghress, May 24, 2011, https://www.maghress.com/marayapress/7025.

communications minister framed the movement as an extremist group fighting against reforms that are the "people's will" and declared, "Islamist and leftists [of the F20] have nothing to do with these democratic reforms." The minister went on to single out the JCO as "exploiting the movement for its own ends."[19] Similarly, Moncef Belkhayat, a former government minister, claimed on national TV that "the concessions have so far been more than enough" and that "there is an institutional process in progress and they [the F20] have to comply" (Idrissi 2012). In essence, the message sent by government loyalists online, and now on national television, was that the F20 was not respecting the democratic process by continuing protests. A cofounder of the F20 argues that reforms in conjunction with the repression experienced in May greatly weakened the movement: "In February, March, and April, the street was powerful and always full of masses. But there was repression in May, and when the movement got back to the streets it was weaker than before. The discussions [in F20 committee meetings] were regarding how to remake the rules of the game to deal with the new constitution. Therefore, the passing of the new constitution [July 1] weakened the movement because the basic purpose of the movement had been hijacked and not clear."[20] The cofounder, along with many journalists and F20 activists, confirmed the common sentiment that the regime's decision to violently repress protests in popular neighborhoods was ultimately to prevent the lower classes from joining the movement:

> When the protesters go to popular neighborhoods, Akib al-Mansoor or Akkari, the state increases repression for two reasons. The first reason is that they are far away from the media outlets and the state channels, and, second, the state does not want protests to enter and mix with popular neighborhoods because they don't want the poor people to know that there is a social movement that wants better living conditions, health, and social justice. So, it means that this part [of society], which does not know about the F20 other than through the state media outlets, which

19. "Rabat Accuses Islamists of Influencing the February 20 Youth Movement," Maghress, May 24, 2011, https://www.maghress.com/chaabpress/3477.

20. F20 cofounder, interview by the author, Oct. 25, 2016, Casablanca.

portray the movement as foreign agents and sexual deviants, will see other types of youth which do not fit in this picture the state portrays. It would lead to an alliance between the movement and these people, and the state sees that this unification would lead to the state losing.

Similarly, F20 activists viewed the imprisonment of Mouad Belaghouat (known as El-Haqed, or "The Enraged"), a rap artist and outspoken critic of the king who was heavily involved in the F20, as a message to the lower classes:

> There were people put in jail, like the rapper El-Haqed—three times [laughs]. I asked myself why they [the regime] chose El-Haqed as an example of repression. It is because he comes from a poor neighborhood where he really made the whole neighborhood sympathize with the movement and with the ideas of the Left. . . . So, it was dangerous for the state. I live in a higher-class neighborhood, and I am therefore not a danger for the regime. They [the regime] know that I can talk a lot [laughs] for hours. There are red lines, but it is not as risky as for a kid who comes from a poor neighborhood and that has a lot of charisma and can make a whole neighborhood rise up. This is what they [the regime] are scared of.

As we see, the regime strategically repressed protesters after major reforms were announced, which led to contentious internal discussions within the F20. Conflicts erupted between reformists and more revolutionary elements about where protests should be held and what the demands of the movement should be. Leading up to May 2011, discussions and conflicts ensued about whether to go into popular neighborhoods. The divide was among members who wanted more extreme change (for example, DWP, JCO), and those who remained reformist in their demands (USP, independents).[21] In Agadir, a major coastal tourist destination, reformists feared that going into popular neighborhoods would result in repression and make the movement look violent; however, the JCO and the DWP, which wanted even more radical changes, did move protests into Agadir's

---

21. F20 cofounder, interview by the author, Oct. 6, 2016, Casablanca.

popular neighborhoods and were indeed met with state violence in May 2011.[22] Similarly, in Marrakech only independent F20 activists along with the JCO and the DWP went into the lower-class Ben Youssef Al-Ali neighborhood to protest high electric and water prices and were met with heavy repression.[23] The divide between what activists characterize as reformist monarchists and more revolutionary republicans became more visible after March 2011 and especially leading up to the king's second major announcement concerning the new constitution.

While the king's reforms convinced many that a social movement was no longer needed and gave rise to internal disagreements about how to resonate with the public, harsher repression along with more revolutionary frames permeating the F20 made the public, and some activists, less likely to continue protesting. My interviews revealed that the repression, starting in May 2011, further hurt the movement's momentum.

Internal conflicts within the F20 were exacerbated by regional events. Some F20 activists echoed the public fear of potential instability and violence. In the words of an F20 cofounder, the Libyan and Syrian civil wars "planted a kind of fear in Moroccans since those revolutions failed and those countries burned down. The people here [in Morocco] became thirsty for security and safety."[24] A member from the Amazigh Cultural Movement indicated how repression in conjunction with the images of violence from the Syrian and Libyan civil wars were affecting protest participation: "In the beginning, everything was peaceful, and the regime was peaceful. But when things happened in Libya and Syria, the regime started to become more violent. When they became violent, and the F20 saw what was happening in the region, there was a type of fear among F20 leaders. Some would stop going to F20 committee meetings in Tangier. So, this was a reason for F20's death. The regime became more violent, and it was successful."[25]

Interviewees again and again suggested that the wave of repression in May 2011 was successful not in ending the movement, but in shrinking

22. USFP leader from Agadir, interview by the author, Dec. 13, 2016.
23. F20 leader from Marrakech, interview by the author, Jan. 4, 2017, Marrakech.
24. F20 cofounder, interview by the author, Oct. 1, 2016, Rabat.
25. Amazigh leader, interview by the author, Dec. 8, 2016, Tangier.

the size of the movement by scaring away bystanders and activists from attending protests that the regime framed as against Moroccan interests. In the words of an activist in Agadir, after May, "the movement continued, but there was a lot of repression, and a big lessening in protesters too."[26] Another elite activist claimed that the regional events were used by reformists to convince more revolutionary elements within the F20 to stop or limit protests: "The activists against change said, 'Do you want to be like Libya? Or Syria?' and the regime in Morocco [took advantage of this fear]."[27] This sentiment was echoed by many women within the F20.

A self-identified Marxist-feminist activist from Agadir began advocating for reform after regional violence increased. In her words: "If we would have protested in a chaotic and violent way, then our destiny would be like Libya's. Our situation today would be with half of our youth injured or dead. Or maybe we would have ended up like Iran—a country that is run by extremists."[28] The same interviewee also reflected on how the lessons from Egypt's revolution made some activists reformists: "In Egypt the Muslim Brotherhood took advantage of the situation. The other protesters like Kifaya and the April 23 Movement[29] and the others did not gain, but rather went to prison and the military was back in power. . . . True equality [gender equality] is a leftist demand. Don't tell me that there is an Islamist movement in the world that called for freedom without oppressing the Left. In Iran that is clear."[30] For many feminist activists, the current state of affairs in Morocco is preferable to an Islamist takeover of the state, which is why some feminist F20 activists became more reformist after the regional rise of the Muslim Brotherhood to power in Egypt. One MALI member from Rabat explained that some feminists became supportive of the king's reforms as a way to curb a potential Islamist takeover

26. "Radical Communist" F20 member, interview by the author, Dec. 12, 2016, Agadir.

27. Majlis Dahm leader, interview by the author, Feb. 21, 2017, Rabat.

28. F20 activist, interview by the author, Dec. 12, 2016, Agadir.

29. Both Kifaya and the April 23 Movement in Egypt are secular movements that helped organize protests that led to the Egyptian Revolution of 2011 (Badran 2014).

30. F20 activist, interview by the author, Dec. 12, 2016, Agadir.

of the state: "Some feminists thought that the symbol of modernity is now the king. So, to stop the rise of the Islamists, we have to be on the side of the king."[31] In other words, for many feminists, it is better to maintain the power of the king than risk an Islamist revolution.

A prominent woman USFP leader from Agadir never called for revolution within the F20 and details why, for many women and moderates within the F20, a facade of democracy is preferable to true democracy in Morocco:

> The king said he has limited power, but after all, we realized that was not true. But, you know we are happy that it's not true. Because, if we really applied democracy in Morocco, then the JCO will win and maybe the Salafists will win. The society is very conservative, and people tend to vote for conservatives. . . . When they go to vote, they vote for conservatism and they vote for Islamists, so we think we are lucky that we have a king [laughs]. Because if we did not have a king, all these freedoms would not remain. We will be just like Iran or Saudi Arabia. . . . In Egypt too they prefer a dictator over ISIS or Al-Nusra or terrorism. Even simple Moroccans, if you ask them on the streets if they like "fake democracy" with some freedoms or real democracy with a system like Iran, they will say, "No, no, no, just keep the king. Just let us be free to wear whatever we want, to go wherever we want," and Moroccans appreciate that the country is quiet and stable with no conflicts—they prefer this at any price, even if the price is democracy or even if the price is the king having a lot of money.[32]

According to this self-proclaimed reformist socialist, the F20 should have never gone into the popular neighborhoods, since doing so provoked violence by the state and risked destabilizing the country altogether. This fear of instability was fueled by the regional images of violence broadcast on televisions screens and plastered on newspapers throughout Morocco. The same activist points out that "average Moroccans" prefer to maintain their

31. MALI member, interview by the author, Mar. 13, 2017, Rabat.
32. USFP regional leader, interview by the author, Dec. 13, 2016, Agadir.

liberties and freedoms, but that Islamists are strategic and know how to win elections. Therefore, for some F20 members, even a dictatorial over-take by the military, as we saw in Egypt, was preferable to the true demo-cratic change in the country. This fear of what revolutionary change would look like permeated the F20 committee discussions and led to a more divided movement. These divisions led to the creation of two F20 factions in Agadir—one calling for revolution and the other for reform.

Therefore, in the eyes of the public and some F20 activists, there was less incentive to continue protests that were increasingly being met with violent repression since reforms were already being implemented. Indeed, contrary to the approach taken by other leaders during the 2011 MENA Uprisings, nationwide repression occurred after concessions were offered and public dialogue about a new constitution was occurring throughout the country. Therefore, keeping in mind that the F20 was undergoing a "framing crisis" with some members sticking to reformist frames and others adopting more revolutionary frames, the scenes of violence that ensued during May 2011 did scare the public about where Morocco was heading. As we will see in the next section, the backdrop of regional vio-lence also convinced Moroccans that change through voting booths and not via protests was the most prudent option for the Moroccan public.

"Vote Yes"

All members of the constitutional committee that drafted Morocco's cur-rent constitution were appointed directly by the king. However, a con-sultative body, headed by another adviser of the king, was created and allowed members of the F20 (mainly political parties and labor unions) to have a say in the new constitution. Unfortunately, political parties and civil society organizations that did send their input to the constitutional committee were not able to debate directly with the committee about the details of the constitution and were made aware of the newly proposed constitution on June 16, 2011—a day before the king presented it to the public (Ottaway 2011). According to some activists, this strategic move allowed the regime to present a new constitution that seemingly received input by civil society. Although many within the F20 were not happy with the process, some activists were satisfied with the new constitution. A prominent human rights attorney contributed draft proposals concerning reforming the judiciary to the constitutional committee and was "very happy that 90 percent of his drafts were accepted."[33]

On June 17, 2011, after months of deliberations among members of the constitutional committee, the king presented the details of the constitutional reforms announced on March 9, 2011.[34] The speech started by referencing the "historical" March 9 speech that "received unanimous national support" and was based on suggestions from political parties, civil society groups, and unions. Civil society organizations and unions were allowed to submit requests during the three-month drafting of the constitution. Although most organizations involved in the F20 refused to take part in the process, many activists did admit that allowing civil society and unions to participate in the process was a big change.

The March 9 speech outlined a draft constitution that called for an elected PM from the largest party in parliament and granted the government more executive powers, including granting the prime minister the power to appoint ministers and ambassadors and letting the PM dissolve the lower house of parliament in consultation with the king. Amazigh activists rejoiced that Tamazight, an indigenous Amazigh language, would become an official language alongside Arabic. Furthermore, the draft constitution called for an independent judicial branch and the establishment of a council to fight corruption, and it promoted gender equality. The speech concluded very much like the March 9 speech by reassuring Moroccans that change would occur with their votes. The king made a plea that he would vote yes in the July 1 referendum and that the implementation of the reforms depended on the people's vote.

Two weeks prior to the speech, President Saleh of Yemen narrowly escaped an assassination attempt, and sporadic violence was occurring

33. Prominent human rights attorney, interview by the author, Mar. 13, 2017, Rabat.

34. "Full Transcript of King Mohammed VI's Speech," Morocco Tomorrow, June 17, 2011, http://www.moroccotomorrow.org/full-transcript-of-king-mohammed-vis-speech -june-17-2011/.

throughout Yemen. Moreover, violence and sectarianism were growing in Syria, while Libya was entering a civil war. The speech reminded the public of this regional reality and urged them to vote yes on July 1:

> I therefore call on political parties, trade unions and civil society organizations, which participated freely, from beginning to end, and with a keen sense of commitment, in developing this draft Constitution, to seek to mobilize the Moroccan people, not only for the purpose of voting the draft Constitution, but also to see to it that it is implemented. Indeed, it constitutes the best means for the accomplishment of the legitimate aspirations of our responsible, vigilant young people, and of all Moroccans, who aspire to achieve our shared ambition of building our nation of the solid foundation of tranquility, unity, stability, democracy, development, prosperity, justice, dignity, the rule of law and the institutions-based state. I shall be at the forefront, seeking an optimal implementation of this sophisticated constitutional project which strengthens the foundations of a constitutional, democratic, parliamentary and social monarchy, once the draft Constitution has, by the Grace of the Almighty, been approved by referendum, next July 1st.[35]

Following the concessionary speech, repression was again used. Throughout the MENA, government-paid thugs known as *baltagiya*, along with genuine supporters of the regime, have been used by states to repress opposition.[36] Perhaps the most widely viewed use of *baltagiya* was on the eighth day of the Egyptian Uprising in 2011, when men on camels charged through crowds of anti-Mubarak protesters, beating them with sticks. In Morocco, the *baltagiya* were used when demonstrations would not be controlled or dispersed by national or local security forces. The *baltagiya* would typically use violence against F20 demonstrators or hold their own proregime demonstrations. In Rabat's Takadum neighborhood, the *baltagiya* would hold counterdemonstrations, incite violence, and even

35. "Full Transcript of King Mohammed VI's Speech."

36. Interviewees often used the Egyptian term *baltagiya* to refer to government supporters who engaged in repressive violence against F20 demonstrators.

throw eggs at F20 members. One activist who partook in protest recalls that "they were uneducated and poor youth which would get paid to raise banners against the movement and violence against the movement."[37] The same activist shed light on how the movement was never united behind going into these marginalized neighborhoods:

> In Takadum eggs were thrown at protesters in front of police officers. . . . The F20 tried to be centered in downtown for many months, and then we thought about going to popular neighborhoods. These people thought that raising slogans by people who live in marginalized neighborhoods within popular neighborhoods was a good change of tactics. Later we tried protesting in popular neighborhoods, like Takadum. We were not sure whether to keep protests in one place or to take them to popular neighborhoods or to combine both strategies together. . . . I myself still don't have an answer to this.[38]

Similarly, a JCO activist anticipated violence when protests moved into popular neighborhoods: "When we crossed the 'red lines' for the regime and went into the popular neighborhoods, we knew they would take action. . . . [T]he Makhzen never wanted to be dragged into violence, because we have the right to respond, but we did not call for that. The Makhzen was aware that being trapped in popular neighborhoods would smear its democratic image. So, the way the Makhzen stopped F20 activity in popular neighborhoods was by sending *baltagiya*." The first known widespread use of *baltagiya* occurred after the June 17 speech (Bouhmouch 2011). Three days after the speech, the F20 held a demonstration to reject the referendum, and police along with progovernment *baltagiya* chased, beat, and dispersed protesters. The promonarchy *baltagiya* held signs praising the king and chanted "The people say 'Yes' to the constitution" (Lazare 2011). According to JCO members, these government-paid groups have a history of inciting violence, so the JCO "sent big groups [of JCO members] to protect the shops in the streets, because *baltagiya* have

37. F20 activist, interview by the author, Nov. 23, 2016, Rabat.
38. F20 activist, interview by the author, Nov. 23, 2016, Rabat.

created violence before."[39] The promonarchy *baltagiya* came from impoverished areas and were reportedly paid one hundred Moroccan dirhams each (ten US dollars) to drive throughout Rabat in large vans, sometimes visibly armed with knives and machetes, and chant slogans supportive of the king, the new constitution, and the referendum (Bouhmouch 2011).[40] In Casablanca's improvised Derb Soltane popular neighborhood, F20 activists were forced to move their protests to other areas when they were confronted with hundreds of proregime supporters waving Moroccan flags and pictures of the king (Brouksy 2011). In Tangier's historically restive Beni Mekada, ten thousand demonstrators packed in the neighborhood's tight streets—many carrying empty ballot boxes, symbolizing a fraudulent referendum vote (Karam 2011c). A local labor-union leader from Tangier elaborated on the especially active role that residents of Tangier's popular neighborhoods played in protests: "Beni Mekada is a marginalized neighborhood, and all forms of social injustice are present there: unemployment, lack of social services, drugs. . . . In Tangier there is a huge difference between social classes. For example, in this area [where we had the interview], it looks like a European country, but you don't see the other face of Tangier here: the popular neighborhoods, the poverty, the lack of bare minimum to survive. This had an impact on protests." In all of Morocco's major cities, *baltagiya* helped disperse or prevent protests from entering certain neighborhoods. However, they were also present leading up to the referendum with a message to vote yes. This period coincided with the ongoing media campaign urging all Moroccans—including imams and political parties—to vote yes for the new constitution (Barany 2013).

The F20: The "Spectacle"

Changes in the political structure through state policies (the March and June reform speeches, July referendum vote, and 2011 early elections), in addition to repression and increased violence in Libya and Syria, sparked debates and arguments that affected the internal framing processes of the

39. JCO member, interview by the author, Dec. 28, 2016, Casablanca.
40. See Nadir Bouhmouch's 2011 documentary, *My Makhzen and Me.*

F20. The repression that followed concessions led to a movement that was becoming internally divided and increasingly disconnected from average Moroccans. The F20's lack of a clear and united message would prove to be especially damaging for the movement. Merouan Mekouar notes that since June 2011, "For average citizens, the February 20 Movement was no longer a movement of 'normal citizens,' but a rather strange alliance between the country's far-left parties and non-loyalist Islamists" (2016, 105). This perception was also felt by F20 members and triggered the experimentation of frames and subsequently the internal conflicts we saw beginning in March and April 2011. An independent-leftist activist and theater organizer and actor noted that in Casablanca, the F20 eventually became a spectacle for Moroccans: "I come from the world of theater and spectacles; we became a spectacle for the people. Every week we would go out and every time in fewer numbers, we go on the street and say the same things and the same slogans, and the people watch us as they pass by. We were a spectacle, and the objective was not to be the spectacle."[41] Some suggested that the lack of clarity in framing demands led to a lack of support from the middle and upper classes, which depend on a stable country under the king.[42] The middle class was represented in the F20, especially since most figureheads were from the middle class, and although the F20 was not largely represented by the upper class, there was hope that they could attract some within the upper class. For example, a number of prominent activists, journalists, politicians, and professionals (such as the doctors' union) began supporting the movement. Despite the class makeup of the movement, demanding reforms of the constitution, without specifying what those reforms ought to be, was a weakness that many interviewees expressed. A USP member in Tangier attributes the movement's demobilization, in part, to the lack of clarity in demands caused by the JCO and the DWP, while claiming that the USP had a clear and consistent demand for a future with a monarch from the beginning.[43]

41. Independent activist, interview by the author, Sept. 22, 2016, Mohammedia.
42. UMT and Hizb al-Umma member, interview by the author, Feb. 26, 2016, Tangier.
43. USP member, interview by the author, Feb. 25, 2016, Tangier.

The F20 was initially self-framed as a strictly reformist movement; however, following the king's speeches and especially during the referendum period beginning in June 2011, the F20 struggled to resonate with the public, and this waning interest pushed some to change their demands from calling for reforms to more extreme demands, short of regime overthrow. Interviewees across all ideologies revealed that arguments concerning the "ceiling" of demands, *Saqf al-mutalib*, pervaded F20 meetings. *Saqf al-mutalib* refers to discussions concerning the type of regime the F20 should demand. The literal translation in English is the "ceiling of the demands"; however, discussions surrounding *Saqf al-mutalib* concern "how far demands can go," with the ceiling being the often unsaid: toppling the king and his regime. Although this sentiment may have always existed within certain political organizations, like the Marxist DWP or the Islamist JCO, dialogue concerning pushing demands closer to a revolutionary ceiling started to appear following the regime's concessions and selective repression. The F20 actively tried to silence the voices that openly demanded toppling a king who was popular throughout Morocco. Some believed that this overthrow was the ulterior motive of many within the F20, and, following discussions concerning the "ceiling of the demands," they were more visible to the public. For instance, a USFP leader in Casablanca indicated how this view was prevalent even as the F20 tried to self-censor those individuals who called for overthrow: "Most of them wanted this [overthrow of regime], even though they hid it. For example, during a general assembly, a leader of the Pioneers Party was talking about the way to protest, but soon and by mistake, he started to say, 'We have to topple the regime,' loudly. Then people who were against this issue rose up, and they tried to mend this by saying it was an electronic blunder. . . . We said that this is not our demand and it is not a reform, but this is what devastated the movement."[44] Suspicion about the extremist nature of the F20 made many reformist members uncomfortable with the increasingly revolutionary tones conveyed in protests and meetings. A former leader of AMDH noted that all F20 factions agreed that there were problems in

---

44. USFP leader, interview by the author, Nov. 24, 2016, Casablanca.

Morocco, especially concerning corruption and wealth distribution, but how to solve those problems became a point of contention: "Maybe there was a general agreement on the negative things that we wanted to change, but there was not agreement on what we wanted to replace the system with: 'What is the alternative we wanted?' This question concerning the future of the movement theoretically created new problems."[45]

Therefore, some F20 activists did not accept reformist demands called for regime change, while some suggested leaving the future of the regime type open for discussion. Nevertheless, the JCO and the DWP did not officially call for overthrowing the regime; rather, they simply framed their demands as "letting the people decide" and leaving the ceiling of demands open.[46] This strategy of leaving open the ceiling of demands is not unusual. Movements use abstract and highly subjective frames to maximize resonance with the public, but, in the context of the 2011 MENA Uprisings during which calls for overthrowing the regime elsewhere had led to sectarian strife and violence, vagueness in demands created conflicts within the F20. A cofounder of the F20 clearly demonstrates how political organizations that wanted a republic, or a future without a king, could not directly call for a republic: "Republicans never said [that] 'we want a republic.' They just said, 'We don't want to put a ceiling on our demands.' We let people decide, but we don't want to say that we want a parliamentary monarchy. If we are enough people on the streets, [then] we can ask for more than a parliamentary monarchy, and others said, 'No, we need to be clear, and we need this [to demand a parliamentary monarchy] for the time being.'"[47]

This play on words obscured the red line of questioning the king's sanctity in Morocco, but to the public the message was clear: members in the F20 wanted radical change (regime change), which most in society did not want. Moreover, previously reticent "republicans" were becoming more open

45. Ex-leader of AMDH, interview by the author, Oct. 5, 2016, Rabat.

46. There were individual members from these organizations who did call for the overthrow of the regime, but the leaders of the JCO and the DWP maintained that it was not their demand.

47. F20 cofounder, interview by the author, Oct. 1, 2016, Rabat.

Table 3

The F20's "Revolutionary Republican" Frames, after March 2011

The F20's diagnostic framing *What is the problem?* *Who do we blame?*	*Main problems*: state type, the monarchy *Attribution of blame*: the king and the Makhzen
The F20's prognostic framing *How to solve the problem?*	*Solutions to the problem*: replace the monarchy with a democratic republic; remove the king
The F20's motivational framing *How do we frame the movement* *and motivate people to join?*	*Frames*: "The people want to overthrow tyranny," "Makhzen get out. Down with despotism," "The people want to overthrow the dictatorship," and "People want the downfall of the regime"

˙These motivational frames tended to highlight the severity of regime corruption and lack of democracy, while also linking their causes to the events in Tunisia and Egypt in order to highlight the urgency to protest and "take advantage" of achieving goals during the protest wave engulfing the Arab world.

about their revolutionary intentions. Table 3 shows the frames adopted by the "revolutionary republicans" within the F20 following the king's March 9 speech. As we can see, those frames adopted by revolutionary republicans differed greatly from the initially reformist frames of the F20.

The change in diagnostic frames shifted blame toward the king, and the solution (prognostic framing) was the overthrow of the regime and by extension the king. Although only the more revolutionary elements of the F20 adopted these frames, in the eyes of reformist F20 activists, the damage was done. By June, the press often covered the F20's internal arguments about the ceiling of demands and frequently speculated about the extremist nature of the JCO. The June issue of the widely read magazine *Tel Qel* covers the internal "radicalization" of the F20 and shows a picture of an activist's sign reading: "I want the overthrow of the regime."[48] An interview in June 2011 with the JCO's deputy secretary-general, Omar

48. *Tel Qel*, issue 477, published June 2011.

Amkasu, questioned whether the JCO's ulterior motive was to overthrow the regime, to which Amkasu vaguely responded that the group wanted to "overthrow corruption and tyranny." Amkasu is also asked to address extreme statements by some JCO members, including a JCO member caught on video stating that "the streets will be cleansed by the blood of the protesters."[49]

The F20's goals and the JCO's motives even sparked talks within the PJD, an Islamist political party. A PJD member of parliament (MP), who in February 2011 did support the F20 and participated in its protests, expressed the concern that members in his party along with the general public had about the ulterior motives of the F20: "We began to ask, what do these people [the F20] want? Do they want reforms of the king's regime and become more democratic? Or do these people want a different political regime?"[50] In the view of many interviewees, this lack of a unified frame along with the conflicts they caused was one of the main reasons for the F20's demobilization. Leftist cofounders of the F20 attempted to quell people's fears about the extremist elements within the F20 by holding press conferences that declared the ceiling of the movement's demands was for reforms and a parliamentary monarchy (a future with a king).[51] However, when leftists spoke on behalf of the F20 in early June 2011, and limited demands to reforms, some members of the JCO became convinced that the movement no longer represented them: "The problem increased after some of the statements of the leaders from the Left; there were public media statements on the roof of demands should be a parliamentary monarchy. This is the point that I said we should end our participation."[52] Similar accounts were found among members of the DWP: "I personally thought that demanding a parliamentary monarchy was a political signal because it limited our demands."[53] The USFP represented one of the

49. Maghress, https://www.maghress.com/hibapress/48761.

50. PJD MP, interview by the author, Feb. 23, 2017, Rabat.

51. "February 20 Movement in Rabat: The Ceiling of Demands Has Not Been Raised," *Hespress*, June 2, 2011, https://www.hespress.com/politique/32431.html.

52. JCO member, interview by the author, Nov. 16, 2016, Meknes.

53. Al-Naj member, interview by the author, Oct. 13, 2106, Rabat.

only parties in the F20 that had previously participated in parliament and worked for change through the system of existing institutions. Naturally, calls to not limit demands to reforms or a future with a king made the USFP question its future in the movement and eventually led to its decision to leave the F20 in April 2011 and encourage its members to vote yes in the July referendum. A party leader in Casablanca made it clear that his party was not comfortable with the new prognostic frame experiment surrounding the ceiling of demands:

> There was within the movement those who called for toppling the regime, and this was not among the F20's demands. Rather, the demand was a parliamentary monarchy, which means that the powers are not centered to the king, not an absolute executive monarchy. If you [referring to the JCO and DWP] want to topple the regime, then you should protest within a certain political party or organization away from the movement of people [the F20]. . . . [I]f you do such protest on behalf of the rest of the F20 movement, it means you crossed the red line.[54]

Another USFP leader similarly thought that, in spite of the vagueness of the JCO's demands, their real intentions were clear: "As the moderate Left, we just want to change the constitution, stop corruption, and change some corrupted leaders. The JCO, you know, they want different things— [they want] revolution."[55] A member of parliament from the Democratic Confederation of Labor, a labor union that is close to the DWP, also expressed concern that extending demands too far would not resonate with Moroccans: "We clashed with them [the DWP] about the constitution we wanted. Almost all of the leftist parties agreed on fighting for a parliamentary monarchy, because the monarchy in Morocco has a history and there are Moroccans who believe that the monarchy is very important for the continuation of life." The same MP expressed concerns about how Islamists felt empowered after the regional rise of Islamists to positions of power in Tunisia and Egypt in October 2011 and January 2011,

---

54. USFP member, interview by the author, Nov. 24, 2016, Casablanca.
55. USFP leader, interview by the author, Dec. 13, 2017, Agadir.

respectively: "After what happened in Tunisia and Egypt, we understood that they wanted everyone to go to the streets and overthrow the regime, and afterward they would gain from that since they were the most organized group. The JCO paid attention to Egypt and Tunisia and, of course, Libya, Syria, and Yemen. But the most important ones [for them] were the developments in Tunisia and Egypt because they [Egyptians and Tunisians] got a new constitution and won governments." The MP was most worried about how discussions concerning the "ceiling of the demands" would ultimately benefit the JCO: their organization is like a military. So, of course, this topic about "the type of state we want" was not up for discussion.[56] The USP also felt that the JCO, especially, had an ulterior motive to overthrow the monarchy and establish an Islamist caliphate, perhaps one reason the JCO insisted on having vague demands.[57]

The vagueness in the JCO and the DWP's new prognostic frame as simply "not limiting the F20's demands" created conflicts within the movement. The alliance between a Far-Left party (DWP) and an illegal Islamist party (JCO) also opened old wounds for many leftist activists within the F20, as well as members of the PJD. Various interviewees indicated that a divide within the F20 occurred between April and May 2011, when an alliance between the JCO and the DWP was formed. To understand this division and why it was so contentious, it is imperative to understand that the alliance between the JCO (Islamist) and the DWP (Marxist) did not sit easily with many leftists because, in their view, Islamists are innately incompatible with liberal democratic ideals. One leftist F20 member, for example, could not understand why the DWP would align itself with an Islamist group that would oppress leftists: "How is it possible that it cooperates with a group that is unjust. If the JCO came into power tomorrow, they would start the killing and repression and oppressing leftist activists. I mean, at a specific point, this contradiction created an ideological problem for many activists."[58] Although the discussions concerning desired

56. CDT MP, interview by the author, Jan. 13, 2017, Rabat.
57. USP member, interview by the author, Feb. 25, 2017, Tangier.
58. Talea member, interview by the author, Dec. 8, 2016, Rabat.

regime type were not necessarily ideologically based, the alliance between Islamists (JCO) and radical leftists (DWP) made many leftists uncomfortable with the alliance. Furthermore, these ideological divisions seemed to seep into the F20's organizational structure, with certain groups dominating certain councils and committees. These internal cleavages led to perceptions by leftists that Islamists were attempting to control the movement by co-opting F20 committees.

Conclusion

Repression was timed to occur after a perceived sense of true change was happening in Morocco. This dynamic led to a lessening in protests and caused the public to become fearful of increasing violence that was exemplified by the civil war in Libya. The scenes of violence in Morocco's popular neighborhoods further frightened Moroccans. An elite USP leader made it clear that regional instability and sectarianism directly affected the movement:

> People were more scared of sectarianism after what happened in Libya and began occurring in Syria. But people were against violence. It was not possible for people to arm themselves. So, what did the regime do? They would say that the JCO wanted the caliphate and would be violent and the DWP is a revolutionary organization and wants the dictatorship of the proletariat. They had a big propaganda campaign, and many people believed this and did not go to the streets. So, people were scared, and also religious slogans began to be chanted, which contradicts the initial agreement.[59]

By June 2011, the options for Moroccans wanting change were to either accept the king's concessions or continue to participate in street protests that were increasingly turning violent and risk destabilizing the country. Most Moroccans opted for the first option, especially considering the king's record of unprecedented reforms in the past. Following concessions and then repression, the F20 found it difficult to recuperate and maintain

59. Majlis Dahm leader, interview by the author, Feb. 21, 2017, Rabat.

a unified and effective message.[60] More important, for many in Morocco, change was already occurring via the king's concessions, and, therefore, the F20 had exhausted its purpose. Ahmed Benchemsi, the founder of the Moroccan magazine *Tel Qel*, summarizes what by mid-May was the common perception of the F20 in Morocco: "Moroccans were getting used to protests—and perhaps bored by their apparent pointlessness—after all, the Constitution was being reformed, wasn't it?" (2014, 220). Ultimately, with the F20 unable to agree on new ways to mobilize supporters, the regime's increasingly harsh response to protests, and the movement's revolutionary and extremist tone becoming increasingly visible, Moroccans chose the former.

A secondary finding of this chapter is that the timing and aim of repression matters. Repression against protests is typically aimed at immediately dispersing protests. In Morocco, however, the primary goal of repression was to delegitimize and fracture a social movement, and direct repression was thus timed to occur when the movement "exhausted its purpose."[61] Again, repression by security forces was used to disperse and, at times, deter demonstrations from occurring in certain areas. The initial smear campaigns, which began days after the F20's initial call to protest in February 2011, along with the calculated use of *baltagiya*, following the March 9 speech, were aimed at sending signals to a public that was all too aware of the regional uprisings and the potential for instability and violence.

60. Benford and Snow find that "movement actors are viewed as signifying agents actively engaged in the production and maintenance of meaning for constituents, antagonists, and bystanders or observers" (2000, 613).

61. JCO leader, interview by the author, Oct. 31, 2016, Rabat.

4

Elections

Using Opposition to Demobilize a Social Movement

Hassan agreed to meet me for a short interview at the University of Rabat. We ended up meeting in the university cafeteria. Hassan is an MP in the House of Councilors and a prominent member of the Party of Justice and Development. Hassan was accompanied by two other well-dressed colleagues who waited a few tables away while I asked my questions. He seemed to have forgotten what I was investigating and asked me what the topic was about. Hassan immediately told me: "I am not a member of the February 20 Movement." Throughout the interview, Hassan, who is one of the more critical voices of the palace within the PJD, emphasized the positive impact of the March 9 speech and the reforms that followed: "The March 9 speech was an encouraging political response, and smart. . . . I was personally happy that this achievement—[it addressed] the most important part of the F20's demands." He was surprisingly straightforward about how the movement helped the PJD win the government: "The protests are what led people to vote for the PJD, because of the people. If this movement offered an alternative option, then the people would not have voted for a second time for the PJD." The end of the interview focused on whether the movement accomplished its goals. Hassan believed that the F20 "came with a mission, and it succeeded in accomplishing. . . . It is a protest dynamic that sent messages to people, and it was received by the smart people, among them the monarchy, and it led to constitutional reforms." After I thanked him for his time, he walked over to the other two men waiting for us to finish and remarked that "we remembered the February 20 Movement!" All three laughed as they left the cafeteria.[1]

Using Opposition to Demobilize

Within the MENA region before 2011, governments allowed Islamist parties to run for local and national elections, but they never allowed them to take control of parliament (Wegner 2011). The case of Morocco demonstrates how the regime successfully used early elections and, more important, the victory of the PJD to demobilize protests. Benchemsi notes that the PJD rode off the F20's wave of protests toward a parliamentary victory and that it benefited not only the PJD but also the regime (2014, 229). Indeed, the PJD never officially supported the F20 protests, although some PJD members did participate in demonstrations. The youth section of the PJD, Baraka, did initially participate in the movement, allowing the PJD to have leverage in the streets before controlling state institutions.[2] Hassan revealed how the party viewed potential PJD involvement with the F20:

> There were discussions within the PJD. Of course, the political culture of the PJD is a culture of working within the institutions and not through pressure from the street. Historically, that is how it works. However, this did not forbid some of its people from going to the streets as individuals and not through the party's decision. Of course, those who went to the streets to protest demanded reforms, and those that did not protest also demanded reforms through social dialogues or statements or books. Prime Minister Benkirane had organized big discussions during that time and demanded approximately those same things that the F20 was demanding. But not through the path of the streets [protests]. Later, there was a general fear that affected these protests through the determination of the political regime and the threat to stability. Therefore, this was considered a type of adventure and a path to the unknown, so this was what Benkirane would say.[3]

1. PJD MP, interview by the author, Feb. 23, 2017, Rabat.
2. Journalist and F20 independent, interview by the author, Nov. 23, 2016, Rabat.
3. PJD MP, interview by the author, Feb. 23, 2017, Rabat.

However, following the king's March 9 speech, Abdelilah Benkirane's reaction embodied the PJD's clear break from the F20's policy to boycott the elections: "The PJD is satisfied. This development looks more like a revolution and the concerned parties are asked to work seriously to make the contents of the speech become a reality" (quoted in Alianak 2014, 113).

Prior to the 2011 MENA Uprisings, the Moroccan regime attempted to keep the PJD out of important positions of power. Opposition-party MPs, like Hassan and Mostafa Ramid, known as "reformists" within the PJD, became much more concessionary toward the palace after the 2011 elections (Mekouar 2016, 105). Since the PJD has never been allowed to form a government and win a plurality in general elections, the 2011 victory of the PJD was an unprecedented victory for Morocco's main opposition party. Activists were cognizant of this reality. In the words of a JCO member from Marrakech: "We don't say the PJD won; rather, we say, 'The king allowed them to win.'" A MALI member in Rabat shared a similar opinion about a PJD-palace pact: "The palace used the PJD to calm the streets down."[4] As we will see, the 2011 victory of the PJD in national general elections played a major role in quelling protests.

Following reforms, the victory of the PJD in 2011 signaled to the public, and some F20 activists, that change had occurred. In essence, some activists and the public tended to believe that a protest movement for change was unavailing.[5] The rise of Islamists into power following the 2011 MENA Uprisings is viewed as a threat to power holders (Bradley 2012; Prashad 2012; Dawisha 2013; Israeli 2017); however, in Morocco, the state stability rested on the Islamist parliamentary victory. Activists asserted that the PJD parliamentary win in 2011, in conjunction with the March 9 speech and the 2011 referendum campaign, signaled to Moroccans that major reforms were being carried out and that street politics via a social movement was no longer necessary. Indeed, the "elections in November

4. MALI member, interview by the author, Mar. 13, 2017, Rabat.

5. According to Little, Tucker, and LaGatta, elections send signals to the public that may affect "whether to take anti-regime action" (2015, 1144).

2011 were perceived by many analysts as a critical test of public confidence in the king's reform agenda" (Arieff 2013, 3).

Social movement theorists tend to classify repression and problem depletion as "killing from the outside"; in other words, they are tactics, often implemented by the state, that deplete social movements (Davenport 2015, 37). Problem depletion refers to lack of relevance (for the public) of claims made by a movement (26). The king initiated a series of concessions—beginning with the March 9 speech—that convinced activists and bystanders to no longer support the movement. In this chapter, I show that the results of the 2011 general election formed part of the regime's concessionary strategy and further depleted the F20's raison d'être. The November 2011 general elections signaled to the public that the king would actually implement reforms announced in March 2011. More important, the victory of an opposition Islamist party depleted the F20's key demand of free and fair elections. Following ideological divides and framing conflicts, the 2011 election results further demobilized an already fractured movement. As we will see, the results of the 2011 parliamentary elections furthered the perception that the F20's demands had been met and that there was no longer a need for protests and changed the incentives of Moroccans to join protests. The outcome of the elections contributed to demobilization because of two important conditions: the PJD had not been "given" a chance to govern prior to the 2011 MENA Uprisings, and the PJD was perceived as the only uncorrupted party among all other competing political parties.[6]

The PJD victory affected the F20's momentum, first, by changing activists' and bystanders' incentives to participate in protests. More specifically, the PJD victory depleted the necessity for street protests, since it signaled to the public that the reform process initiated on March 9, 2011, was culminating in unprecedented change. Importantly, it was the fact that the PJD won a parliamentary plurality, and not that early elections

6. The PJD has always brought the issue of corruption to the forefront of its agenda and has focused on transparency and anticorruption policies (Mekouar 2010, 7).

were held, that convinced activists to stop protesting. Second, the PJD victory had a divisive effect within the F20. Activists who were supportive of the election results were accused of being co-opted by the regime. Finally, the JCO officially stopped supporting F20 protests just two weeks after the PJD won the 2011 general elections. Both the PJD victory and the JCO departure are viewed by activists as the most palpable blows to the movement. It was only after these events that we saw an immediate halt in all major F20 protest activity. Leftists accuse the JCO of withdrawing from the F20 since fellow Islamists (the PJD) were in power. However, JCO members ardently reject this assertion and attribute their decision to leave the F20 to internal conflicts. We will see how the F20's structure may have also pushed the JCO toward withdrawing from the movement.

The Signaling Role of Authoritarian Elections

The electoral victory of 2011 sent signals to the public that the king was devolving some powers and heeding a movement's demands. Previous studies focusing on the informational role of elections have focused on how elections ensure regime strength. This section will outline how a semiauthoritarian[7] regime can use elections to demonstrate a devolution of power—not regime strength. It need not imply that an actual devolution of power is occurring. Rather, if a party that is not controlled or closely aligned with the regime forms a government, it signals to the public that power sharing is occurring with the ruling regime. This signal also tells the public that the traditionally reformist king is, again, listening to the people's demands. This perceived faith in reforms is accomplished not solely by holding elections but by allowing certain opposition parties to take control of parliaments—thus signaling unprecedented change.

Elections play an informational role, which affects activists' and bystanders' propensity to protest. As Little, Tucker, and LaGatta note, "Public signals (like an election result) could serve as a focal point

---

7. I use the term *semiauthoritarianism* since Morocco allows opposition parties to operate relatively freely and compete in elections, even though (prior to 2011) they are usually not permitted to form governments or win parliamentary pluralities. See Ward 2009; and Olcott and Ottaway 1999.

determining whether citizens protest or not" (2015, 1144). According to Little, "Elections generate public information about the relative strength and popularity of the incumbent leaders, which affects the behavior of the leaders as well as other elites and the general population" (2012, 250). Therefore, since elections, according the Little, can affect whether citizens protest, incumbents who do poorly in elections are more likely to offer concessions that lessen the chance of protests (Little 2012). On the other hand, if an incumbent does well in an election, then they will try to consolidate power (Little 2012).

Scholars have theorized that elections within authoritarian contexts play a variety of functions. Some researchers find that elections are intended to signal the incumbent's popularity (Cox 2009; Little 2012; Rozenas 2012; Little 2015). Others emphasize that elections are "survival mechanisms for incumbents, as patronage distribution networks between candidates and constituents, and as performances broadcasting state might" (Brownlee 2012, 808). For example, Blaydes (2010) argues that former Egyptian president Hosni Mubarak used elections to allocate rents to elites by revealing information concerning the loyalty of bureaucratic officials and party cadre, which in turn allowed authoritarian leaders to make decisions about appointments. Other scholars find that authoritarian elections help power holders know where to allocate public goods and services (Baldwin 2005; Lust-Okar 2006; Magaloni 2006; Ortega and Penfold-Becerra 2008).

Some scholars focus on the signals that electoral fraud sends to a public during elections. Simpser (2013) shows that electoral fraud signals the repressive capacity of the state. Electoral fraud can also push individuals to overcome the collective-action problem to work together for change (Tucker 2007). Simpser also argues that manipulation can "discourage opposition supporters from turning out to vote or to protest" (2013, 3). Similarly, certain types of visible electoral fraud, like nullifying ballots, does have a signaling effect that makes incumbents look stronger (Little 2012, 2015). According to Little (2015), within a context where fraud is expected, the corrupt incumbent looks stronger when fraud is exposed by international monitors. Thus, not engaging in fraud is a signal of weakness within noncompetitive elections where citizens expect some level of fraud to take place. In another study, Little, Tucker, and LaGatta conclude that public reports of election fraud will lead to higher probabilities and levels of protests because if an incumbent needs massive fraud to win an election, then it signals that "enough citizens dislike the regime," which can incentivize protesters (2015, 1143).

Finally, other conventional findings contend that when all political parties perceive that they have an opportunity to win elections, civil conflicts will be less likely to occur (Przeworski 1991; Weingast 1997). In relation to Morocco, this wisdom may explain why an opposition party, like the PJD, has consistently decided to compete in elections but did not officially partake in F20 demonstrations. Although the PJD, like other Islamists in the region, participated in elections without winning pluralities, the formal inclusion of the PJD in elections "has enabled the PJD to increase its organizational capacities, to broaden its support remarkably, and to impact directly on the agenda setting of existing political organizations" (Albrecht and Wegner 2006, 136). Since the PJD's inception, the specter of state repression loomed over the party; therefore, the PJD carefully gained parliamentary seats since 1997 and pushed for policy changes through institutions. The same fear of repression persisted under the current king's reign. For example, the party was fearful that the king would use the 2003 Casablanca terrorist attack as an excuse to ban the party altogether (Willis 2014, 148). Since 1997, the PJD has attempted to reframe itself as a moderate Islamist party that could cooperate with other parties and ideologies within parliament (Wegner 2011). In essence, prior to the 2011 MENA Uprisings, the PJD was making incremental gains within the existing political system.

The literature has yet to explain why protests lessen when previously sidelined parties win elections in authoritarian contexts. More specifically, existing theories do not explain why the victory of certain opposition political parties would convince activists to cease protesting. Some scholars emphasize a link between social unrest and a change in the character of political parties. Londregan and Vindigni (2008) argue that free elections can forestall conflict by revealing the strength of factions and therefore discourage violent civil war. In general, however, the link between authoritarian elections and demobilization is underdeveloped. Current studies focus on how authoritarian elections affect opposition parties, while they overlook how elections affect the momentum of existing protests. Moreover, studies concerning authoritarian elections and protests have focused on the role that the fraud plays in affecting the likelihood of protests, but not in decreasing and demobilizing ongoing protests. This book departs from these studies by shifting focus from political parties to existing protest movements. This chapter does not seek to explain why a political party rationally chooses to partake in elections or street politics, but rather it examines why the electoral victory of certain opposition parties may quell existing protest movements.

Therefore, this chapter focuses on the relationship between ongoing protest movements and elections, while also shedding light on when authoritarian regimes may want to signal that they are devolving their power. As Brown notes, authoritarian regimes use elections to manage opposition and ensure favorable electoral outcomes. This quelling of opposition is done, according to Brown, "through drawing and redrawing the rules, district boundaries, access to media, and other features of the electoral process" (2012, 23). Authoritarian regimes allow opposition groups to run in elections, but they successfully limit them from winning and forming governments. During times of social unrest, however, authoritarians may do just the opposite: allow opposition parties to win. Heeding a protest movement's demands for democratic reform, specifically by allowing the unprecedented election of opposition parties, can directly affect a protest movement's momentum. For movements that are reformist in nature, electoral success by the opposition signals to activists and the public that power holders are listening to demands and going through with reforms, and they no longer need a social movement for change.

For an opposition party's parliamentary victory to lessen ongoing protests, the party needs to be independent of authoritarian rulers, perceived by the public to be uncorrupted, and never held a parliamentary plurality or majority. Demonstrating to the public that true change is occurring sends important signals that contentious politics are no longer needed. The election of opposition parties is not always a signal of true changes, specifically when the political party is perceived to be an extension of the regime. Authoritarian regimes usually use the electoral victories of loyalist parties to avoid opposition majorities or pluralities within the national legislature. In the case of Morocco, not all electoral outcomes would have had the same effect on the F20. For one, some political parties are inherently co-opted since they were created by the regime (for example, PAM), while other parties have been co-opted over time by the regime (Istiqlal). Neither the electoral victory of regime loyalist nor co-opted parties would be able to credibly signal to the public, and to the protest movement itself, that true change was under way.

Thus, even if the government holds early elections and announces reforms, the election of royalist parties will not curb ongoing street protests. If, for example, a royalist party held a parliamentary majority in the past, and is reelected during times of social protest, protests will not lessen. Deprivation theory claims that some movements occur when people feel that they are deprived of goods, services, resources, or rights (Gurr 2015; McAdam, McCarthy, and Zald 1988). If we accept deprivation theory and assume that social movements occur when groups of people feel deprived of something they feel entitled to (in this case more democracy), then the election of royalist parties will not likely signal to a public that democratic change has occurred. This lack of perceived change, in turn, will not curb a social movement's incentive to continue protests.

Finally, the public needs to believe that the political parties are not co-opted by the regime. As mentioned, various opposition parties within the MENA eventually became co-opted by authoritarian regimes. In contrast, my interviewees believed the PJD was clean and uncorrupted. The perception that an opposition party will remain un-co-opted signals to the public that power holders are committing to reforms. Furthermore, the public is less likely to trust an opposition party that has been marred by corruption scandals, because it may be easily co-opted by the regime. In the words of one interviewee, some F20 leftists voted for the PJD during the 2011 parliamentary elections precisely because they were a "transparent and moral party," which "did not take the path of previous corrupt parties."[8] The PJD

8. Journalist and F20 participant, interview by the author, Nov. 23, 2016, Rabat.

was the only party during the 2011 elections that fulfilled the three afore-mentioned conditions.

In relation to the MENA region, Islamists have been the leading oppo-sition parties. In spite of this situation, when Islamist parties in the past have garnered many seats (or a majority), regimes have canceled elections (1991–92 Algerian legislative election), used increased repression (Egyp-tian presidential elections of 2005), and used electoral laws to ensure Islamists do not win pluralities or majorities (Morocco and Jordan) (Weg-ner 2011). In the words of Brown: "Elections are freer because they include more serious contestants. But they are not fair, because only incumbents can win" (2012, 2). Quite simply, as Brown notes, the MENA regimes allowed Islamists to run, but they never allowed them to win positions of power: "In many Arab countries, the most reliable and stable electoral rule is that the opposition cannot win. But Islamists run even though losing is foreordained. Actually, they go further: they generally do not even contest a majority of seats. Islamist leaders turn the necessity of losing into a vir-tue, citing the slogan 'participation not domination'" (6).

Like other Islamists within the MENA, the PJD did not expect to win elections, but they participated nonetheless to expand the party's organi-zational capacities and support base. Albrecht and Wegner note that the PJD was "anticipatorily obedient" to the palace for not contesting election results or contentious legislation (2006, 133). The PJD was an opposition party that avoided crossing red lines drawn by the palace. For instance, after the 2003 Casablanca terrorist attack by Islamist militants, the PJD decided to no longer criticize a proposed law that would equate "public disturbance" with terrorism (Wegner 2006, 133). Besides fearing repres-sion, the PJD did not cross red lines (that is, challenge the king's authority) since they achieved their goal of "strengthening their political base" by taking in supporters from other (illegal) Islamist organizations, like the JCO (Boukhars 2010, 129). Whether the PJD would support F20 protests during 2011 was, naturally, a question many Moroccans asked.

The king, argues Abdel-Samad, could use only limited repression during the 2011 MENA Uprisings in order to maintain the palace's close relations with the United States and Europe, as well as its image of a democratizing nation and, therefore, "decided that the main tool to contain the demands it faced would be to increase access to the political system in order to institutionalize them [demands for reform]" (2014, 804). Abdel-Samad believes that reforms and the ratification of the new constitution on July 1, 2011, lessened the F20's momentum, not the PJD's electoral victory. Although this point is an important factor in mitigating dissent, it did not end the F20's activity. Rather, as I argue here, the 2011 election results sent signals to the public that reforms were being implemented, which resulted in declining protest activity. The Moroccan case shows that winning parliamentary elections can be mutually beneficial for regimes and Islamist parties: Islamist parties win control of parliaments, while regimes assuage pressure from the streets.

In Morocco, the 2011 "Vote Yes" referendum campaign and, more important, the unprecedented victory of a nonroyalist opposition party—the PJD—in parliamentary elections signaled to the public that the king was devolving his powers with a new constitution and that reforms had been implemented. My interviews reveal that these signals, in turn, facilitated the F20's demobilization by changing the incentives of ordinary citizens to join protests. The election results further affected the F20 because the results convinced some movement activists to abandon their protests because the public stopped supporting the movement. My interviews revealed that when uncorrupted and nonroyalist parties win elections, the public believes that the government is implementing their previously declared reforms and taking steps toward democratic change, thus invalidating the necessity of a social movement.

Opposition Islamists and Royalist Parties

In 1962, King Hassan II allowed Morocco to become a multiparty system while also granting himself and future kings the title *amir almouminin* (commander of the faithful), a position that grants the king guardianship and control over religion in Morocco (Hissouf 2016, 46). Today, much like under Hassan II's rule, an array of political parties coexist with a powerful monarch that uses his position to promote, limit, or outright ban certain parties that do not accept the king's title as *amir almouminin*. John Waterbury's formative analysis of Moroccan segmented politics elaborated on the system of multiparty control that persists today: "Once having assumed the arbiter function, a few simple principles have guided monarchical conduct. First, no group may be permitted to become too strong, and to counter hegemonic tendencies life is breathed into rival groups. On the other hand, no group (and this includes the opposition parties) may be permitted to die utterly" (1970, 148). The Authenticity and Modernity Party (PAM) was controversially created in 2008 by a close adviser and former classmate of the king, Fouad Ali al-Himma.[9] The propalace party PAM was formed in response to the increasing Islamist PJD representation in parliament and to counter the general public's disillusionment with party politics and elections. Matt Buehler's interviews with opposition leaders notes that PAM, known as the "King's Party," would often host large "parties in rural areas to buy votes, and drops campaign pamphlets from airplanes. That's clear evidence of regime support." Buehler's interview reveals PAM leaders' embrace of clientelism, with one leader stating that "Moroccans are simple" and that "they'll vote for someone because he provides resources" (2018, 70). With the help of the palace, PAM quickly dominated Moroccan politics through what is known in Morocco as transhumance or changing party allegiance.[10] By 2011, PAM was the newest and most powerful royalist party that was expected to win a plurality of seats. In 2009, PAM merged together five parties and subsequently swept the June 2009 local elections. Although only two years old, PAM controlled 17 percent of the deputies in the lower house and 27 percent in the upper house by October 2010 (Köhler 2010, 11).

During the 2007 parliamentary elections, only 37 percent of the populace voted, since there was "widespread resentments towards the corrupt and self-serving nature of many party politicians" (Willis 2014, 148). Hassan echoed this resentment leading up to February 20, 2011: "PAM represented a big blow to democracy in Morocco, and it was supported

9. "Palace Party Seeks to Dominate the Moroccan Political Scene," Wikileaks, Oct. 28, 2009, https://wikileaks.org/plusd/cables/09RABAT877_a.html.

10. Eva Wegner notes that in Morocco, changing party membership for MPs is a very common phenomenon and that parliament is an arena for co-optation and "self-interested actors" to rise within elite ranks (2011, 18).

by the administration and created a type of frustration among many citizens."[11] This resentment helped the Islamist and seemingly less corrupt PJD increase its representation in parliament. Indeed, in 2009 the PJD and the USFP formed an alliance to prevent PAM from winning some communal elections (Buehler 2018).

The F20 was unified in its opposition to the rise of PAM. In Tangier, F20 protests were aimed specifically at PAM figureheads, which led PAM leaders to flee the country for France.[12] Another F20 activist links the protests of 2011 to the rise of PAM and notes that some protesters called for the ouster of the corrupt secretary-general of PAM:

> It is important to know what the situation before February 20 was like too. It was a dark past. PAM was given all the tools from the government to win. Only 37 percent of people voted in 2007. The regime was surprised by this percentage. . . . People who have a right to register to vote did not vote. . . . When the F20 came, the regime was surprised that activists lifted pictures of corrupt [PAM] politicians who were close to the king. I myself was surprised by the size of protests and the slogans when I was in Rabat.[13]

The F20 demonstrations and general discontent toward PAM culminated in al-Himma's (PAM's founder) resignation from the party. Some speculate that, following palace visits shortly before his departure, al-Himma was forced to resign from politics by the king (Buehler 2013b, 250). Manar Sulaimi, a political scientist at the Mohammed V University in Rabat, claims that the F20 inadvertently helped the PJD win, since it targeted PAM during protests and "made part of public opinion go in another direction [toward the PJD]."[14] Therefore, following increased pressure from the streets and the subsequent resignation of their founder, PAM was greatly

---

11. PJD MP, interview by the author, Feb. 23, 2017, Rabat.

12. USP member, interview by the author, Feb. 25, 2017, Tangier.

13. Hizb al-Umma member, interview by the author, Nov. 5, 2016, Rabat.

14. "Reasons for the Rise of 'Justice and Development' in Morocco," Al-Jazeera, Nov. 28, 2011, http://www.aljazeera.net/news/reportsandinterviews/2011/11/28/أسباب-صعود- العدالة-والتنمية-بالمغرب.

weakened. The damage inflicted on PAM during F20 protests helped pave the way for a PJD win on November 25, 2011. Leading up to the 2011 elections, it was clear that a parliamentary victory for PAM would not have demobilized the F20. Voter apathy during parliamentary elections was a common occurrence in Morocco, and it was largely because royalist and co-opted parties traditionally won pluralities. Indeed, a 2010 survey by the Arab Center for Research and Policy Studies found that only 24 percent of Moroccans were satisfied with their country's political conditions at the time.[15] All competing political parties during 2011, except the PJD, were either royalist or co-opted by the palace. Matt Buehler outlines the long history of the palace co-opting and effectively silencing opposition voices. Buehler details how PAM was used by the palace to co-opt rural politicians especially:

> In one rural commune, Dar Bouazza, the PAM moved to co-opt Abdelkarim Choukri, a mayor from a small opposition party. Heading one of the region's influential families, Choukri controlled many local resources, including two large farms that employed dozens of peasant families. However, as an opposition politician, Choukri could not attract regime resources for economic development. Since he aimed to increase resources available for his rural commune's residents, Choukri embraced the PAM's co-optation. Indeed, he told the party's leaders that he "wasn't a beginner" at elections in rural areas and could mobilize clientelist hierarchies of peasant employees to win votes. (2018, 71)

Buehler notes that PAM also was used by the palace to remove specific opposition politicians by using regime resources. For example, in one instance a regime ally used his ties with the palace to build "water wells and other development projects for the villagers before the election" (72). Moroccans were familiar with these tactics to co-opt and silence opposition.

It is safe to conclude—as John Waterbury did in his analysis of Moroccan politics—that political parties and elections are used by the Moroccan

---

15. See "The Arab Opinion Project: The Arab Opinion Index," Arab Center for Research and Policy Studies.

regime to maintain its grip on power. Indeed, "safety-valve" elections within authoritarian contexts do provide institutional outlets for the opposition to "blow off steam" (Lust-Okar and Jamal 2002; Buehler 2013a). Within the Middle East and North Africa, authoritarian leaders have successfully controlled Islamists by allowing them to compete in local and general elections where, through changing electoral rules or redistricting, their power can be manipulated (Brumberg 2005; Brownlee 2012; Buehler 2013a). Morocco is no exception to this trend. The predecessor of the PJD, al-shabiya al-islamiya al-maghrebiya (the Moroccan Islamic Youth), was founded as a legal association in 1972 in order to counter leftists in Morocco (Willis 2014, 162). The organization was eventually banned after its members were accused of murdering a senior leftist of the USFP. In 1975, the group became more militant and engaged in assassinations and weapons smuggling; however, by the late 1980s, under the command of Abdelilah Benkirane, the group began cooperating with the monarchy. In 1992, "Benkirane's Islamist activists" were integrated "into a small secular political party, the Popular Democratic and Constitutional Movement [MPDC]," which eventually changed their name to the PJD in 1998. Eventually, Islamist activists took over the MPDC "until it made up the organization's governing council, which subsequently voted to change the MPDC's name to the PJD in 1998" (Buehler 2013a, 142).

The PJD was careful not to criticize the political system and voluntarily limited the seats it would run for in the 1997 national elections because of King Hassan II's harsh repression. As Wegner notes, the PJD's fear of repression led the group to aim for "consolidation of inclusion," and this fear was amplified by the regional repression Islamists faced in Algeria, Tunisia, and Egypt (2011, 93). After the 2001 elections, the PJD became the third-largest party in parliament (Willis 2014, 182). During the 2007 elections, it was clear that the PJD would do well and continue its upward trend in gaining parliamentary seats; however, "the party achieved only a modest increase in its representation, leaving it the second largest party in parliament" (183). Willis (2014) argues this moderate increase was the result of low turnout owing to the PJD's failure to distinguish itself from the political system and other parties, which the public had discredited. Nevertheless, the public perception was that the PJD was cheated. Wegner succinctly summarizes the sentiment following the election results: "Even leading pragmatists were convinced that the PJD had been cheated—not only by vote buying, but by some form of regime intervention. The PJD was convinced that it had been denied some seats 'here and there' because ultimately the regime would not tolerate a PJD prime minister. As one party leader put it, the King would have been 'embarrassed' by a PJD prime minister" (2011, 92). Election results were influenced, if not completely controlled, by the government after the 1997 elections (75). The 2009 local elections were no exception to this trend. Since 2009, PJD representation declined from previous years, which was owing to not only the rise of PAM, but also a change in formal electoral rules that disadvantaged the PJD and the selective application of corruption laws aimed at smearing the PJD's image (Buehler 2013a, 140). The PJD was successful, however, in portraying an image of being an alternative to other parties by offering more educated candidates that were not tied to local elites or perceived as corrupt. A study found that 61 percent of PJD candidates "were university-educated compared to only 23% of candidates generally" (Pellicer and Wegner 2015, 39). The authors also found that the PJD's "promises in local elections can be summarized as a higher level of 'proximity' to the voters (being responsive to their demands), to 'moralize the management of public affairs' (less corruption), and to provide improved access to government services" (38). Indeed, where the PJD did gain high support, there was "a substantial increase in investment upon the arrival of the PJD," which suggests that the PJD made good on their promise of improving government services (50). Intissar Fakir echoes some of these reasons that the PJD resonated with Moroccans and adds that the wave of protests started by the F20 helped lead the PJD to victory: "The PJD maintained a degree of comparative credibility that translated into more votes in the polls. Although the party had distanced itself from the February 20 Movement protests, the political openings allowed it to take advantage of its reputation as a relatively less corrupt political actor. Its clear platform, more democratic internal organization, strong grassroots connections, and reputation for relative independence appealed to the populace. Also, its limited government experience was an advantage in this case, given the public's skepticism about traditional political forces" (2017, 5). By the time of the 2011 elections, "the PJD was the only political party which at that time enjoyed a considerable degree of legitimacy vis-à-vis Moroccan voters" (Dalmasso 2012, 219). The PJD was able to leverage F20 protests to its advantage and did threaten to engage in protests (Buehler 2013b). Buehler (2013b) argues that this ultimatum forced the regime to concede to its demands during the 2011 referendum campaign, like freeing one of its political prisoners and even forcing al-Himma to leave PAM. Buehler notes how the PJD used the F20 protests as leverage, including threatening to bring "the PJD's parliamentary members into the streets with the February 20th movement protesters if the Interior Ministry implemented new revisions to the electoral rules, which the Islamists saw as making the system more undemocratic" (2013a, 150). The PJD also threatened to join F20 protests if PAM won the 2011 parliamentary elections.

The national referendum gave the public an outlet to vote for change while also granting the king a chance to deflect attention away from protests. The public was less optimistic about the 2011 general elections, and the PJD's surprise victory of 107 seats demonstrated that there was a clear plurality in parliament by a party that was previously sidelined. Abdelilah Benkirane, who was once a militant that rejected participating in the Moroccan electoral process, became prime minister on November 29, 2011. Both the PJD and the regime benefited from this outcome. Simply put, although the PJD did not invest energy into F20 protests during 2011, they did exploit the benefits of early elections and increased powers to the prime minister.

The 2011 General Election Results: Signaling Change

On July 8, 2011, the cover of the widely read Moroccan magazine *Tel Qel* reflected a common sentiment throughout the nation: change was occurring, but it was not enough. The magazine cover displayed a middle-aged woman in a hijab ominously casting a ballot for the 2011 referendum. The title reads: "Referendum YES, but . . . ," followed by the subheading that reads, "Excessive propaganda and insufficient democratic advances: the constitution of Mohamed VI passes with a very disappointing—yes."[16] The sentiment that democratic advances were occurring was clear, but so too was the sentiment that they were not enough to diminish national discontent. Nevertheless, many citizens were satisfied with the incremental changes taking place, which explains why voter turnout for the referendum vote was just over 72 percent (National Democratic Institute 2011).

Many F20 activists did not expect the PJD to win. Rather, they logically predicted that history would repeat itself and the PJD would not win the government. Some interviewees expected PAM would, again, win and fracture the parliament—leaving it susceptible to co-optation by the regime. A leftist F20 cofounder sounded disappointed that a propalace party, like PAM, did not win. In his words, more revolutionary members "waited for them [the regime] to continue with this strategy [electing a royalist party], and then we would have a true democratic revolution."[17] The same activist outlines why the PJD victory essentially halted the F20's momentum. In fact, for revolutionaries in the movement, this apparent "victory" was viewed as defeat:

> What happened was that the PJD won first place, but they did not just win sixty seats with the second party following with fifty-eight seats. The regime could have managed and manipulated that [result]. Rather, when they came in first place with such a large number of seats, it became clear to the public that there was a big change in the country. It meant that, according to public opinion, there was no need for a social movement like the F20. Therefore, we, the independents of the movement along with the JCO, had the same exact analysis of the situation: we had to end the movement and try different forms of activism in order to change the country. Afterward, the movement was only composed of the extreme Left.[18]

16. *Tel Qel*, issue 480, published July 2011.
17. F20 cofounder, interview by the author, Oct. 26, 2016, Casablanca.
18. F20 cofounder, interview by the author, Oct. 26, 2016, Casablanca.

It is important to note that during the 2002 elections, the PJD-dominated districts were "extensively gerrymandered to its great disadvantage" (Boukhars 2010, 107). Similarly, the 1997 general elections were marred by allegations of vote buying, and international observers claimed that the results were manipulated and even predetermined by the state (Wegner 2011, 75). Therefore, F20 activists were surprised and some were pleased that the regime did not redraw districts or manipulate elections so that a royalist party could win. One F20 activist expressed this sentiment during a protest that occurred a month before the 2011 elections: "It is obvious that the polls will bring to power the same figures who have for years been plundering the wealth of the country and holding hostage the future of the Moroccan population" (Karam 2011b). Considering the public outcry against PAM, it is clear that the victory of PAM would have likely increased contention on the streets. Despite the unprecedented reforms, in 2011 "few Moroccans believed that the elections would usher in a fundamental transformation of the regime" (Lust 2012, 112). This point is clear when looking at the official low turnout of just over 45 percent. Moreover, 20 percent of ballots were invalid or protest ballots, or both.[19] Turnout in 2011 was higher than the 2007 elections (37 percent turnout with 19 percent spoiled ballots), but this slight increase was likely owing to "revisions to the voters' register," where voter cards were not issued; rather, only a national ID card was needed to vote (National Democratic Institute 2011, 7). Contrasting the high turnout for the referendum vote (72.56 percent of eligible voters) and the low turnout in the general parliamentary elections (45.4 percent) suggests that the public wanted change but perhaps had less faith in parliamentary elections. Although there was faith that the constitution would be reformed, there was perhaps more skepticism about whether the PJD would be allowed to win first place. Keeping in mind that throughout the region, including Morocco, Islamists were allowed to participate in elections but never win majorities and pluralities, a PJD win was a signal that real change had occurred. In other words, relatively free

---

19. "Morocco Votes in First Poll since Mohamed VI's Reforms," BBC, Nov. 26, 2011, https://www.bbc.com/news/world-africa-15884484.

and fair elections have occurred in Morocco prior to 2011, but what was different this time was that Islamists could win.

Despite public indifference and a boycott of the elections by the F20, the results of these elections proved to have a very damaging effect on the future of the F20. The PJD came in first place and won a plurality of 107 out of 395 seats within the lower house of parliament, and the promonarchist party Istiqlal (Independence Party) came in a distant second with 60 seats. The remaining parties that competed, including Istiqlal, were generally viewed as already having had an opportunity to govern, as plagued with corruption, or as extensions of the regime's rule. Perhaps the most controversial of these parties was PAM. Similarly, Istiqlal is a monarchist party that had been marred by controversies, so much so that activists during 2011 carried banners demanding the ouster of the previous Istiqlal prime minister, Abbas el-Fassi (Karam 2011a). In the words of a F20 figurehead in Marrakech, "If Istiqlal won [during the 2011 elections], things would have changed because people [activists and ordinary Moroccans] would say that the elections were corrupted."[20] The National Party of Independents, which won 52 seats in 2011, also has close ties to the monarchy and was formed (like PAM) by the brother-in-law of the late King Hassan II. The Socialist Union of Popular Forces has headed the government in the past and formed coalitions with various parties perceived as corrupt—most notably the Abbas el-Fassi government in 2007 (Boukhars 2011). Finally, the Popular Movement (MP) and the Constitutional Union (UC) won 24 and 17 seats, respectively. Both the MP and the UC are royalist parties that are closely allied with the king. In table 4, I outline the percentage of seats won by each party.

Interviewees believed there was a unanimous sentiment among both activists and ordinary citizens that the PJD was the only competing party that could have curbed protests. To be clear, most F20 activists I interviewed were not supportive of the PJD; however, they expressed the common sentiment that only a PJD win during 2011 would have convinced most Moroccans that change was occurring and subsequently quelled protests.

20. F20 leader, interview by the author, Jan. 4, 2017, Marrakech.

Table 4

2011 Election Results

Political Party[*]	Percentage of Seats
Justice and Development Party	27.1
Istiqlal	15.2
National Rally of Independents	13.2
Authenticity and Modernity Party	11.9
Socialist Union of Popular Forces	9.9
Popular Movement	8.1
Constitutional Union	5.8

[*]The remaining parties represented in parliament tend to be less influential parties that garnered 5 percent or less of seats.

As noted by a researcher from Qadi Ayyad University in Marrakech, "Wary of the sweeping change the F20 movement proposed, Moroccans saw in the PJD the most credible political alternative to respond to their claims" (Radi 2017, 47). In the words of a JCO member and F20 activist: "The PJD was the regime's last card," which implied that a PJD win was the only way the king could have peacefully ended the protests.[21] Although the F20 was suffering internal conflicts and protest decline, a hard core of activists—mainly the JCO, the Far Left (most notably the DWP), and independent activists—continued protests. It was only after the PJD victory that major protests stopped and the largest power within the F20, the JCO, withdrew from the streets and the movement.

A leader from the leftist-oriented union the CDT went so far as to claim that the results of the 2011 elections "broke the movement."[22] Even in Tangier, which had the largest F20 demonstrations, protests became smaller "directly after the results of the elections" were announced.[23] When asked what would have occurred had the PJD not won, one F20

21. JCO member, interview by the author, Jan. 5, 2017, Marrakech.
22. CDT leader, interview by the author, Jan. 19, 2017, Casablanca.
23. USP member, interview by the author, Feb. 25, 2017, Tangier.

activist from Casablanca did not hesitate to respond: "Revolution. Revolution. The PJD was the only party that did not participate in government. It was the only way to exit this political crisis."[24] In essence, although the clear majority of F20 activists I interviewed were not supportive of the PJD, many knew that only a PJD win would have led to a lessening of protests.

The reasons behind why there was so much public confidence for change through a PJD win are varied. As mentioned, it was the only opposition party with no direct link to widespread corruption or the regime. Therefore, the PJD's "clean," independent, and nonroyalist position tended to bolster the party's place as a driver of real change. A prominent human rights attorney who helped draft the new constitution of 2011 made it clear that, despite reforms, the "regime needed the PJD to win" and that the "PJD was the only party to not have a shot in government, so it was important that they won, and people wanted to give them a chance."[25] Leftists, which have had an extremely contentious relationship with the PJD, unanimously admitted that this "clean and reformist" image was common among Moroccans: "Most Moroccans thought that the PJD would save them from corruption and so on, and it would reconsider the status of the government institutions. Therefore, people voted for this party. . . . The laymen believed that the PJD would make interesting reforms that it promised during the election campaign and that it would make reforms and reestablish the state of law and justice."[26] Similarly, an Islamist member from Hizb al-Umma believed that "the PJD benefited from the idea that 'we are new, so give us a chance.' So, the people thought 'why not try the PJD,' and they gave them a chance."[27] Others noted that the PJD's Islamic ideology along with their image as an untested and uncorrupted party played a role in public satisfaction with the election results. In other words, "The PJD had a popular discourse, a discourse that played with the imaginations and minds of Moroccans."[28]

24. Independent F20 cofounder, interview by the author, Oct. 26, 2016, Casablanca.

25. Elite attorney, interview by the author, Mar. 16, 2017, Rabat.

26. Talea member from Berkane, interview by the author, Dec. 2, 2016, Rabat.

27. Hizb al-Umma member, interview by the author, Nov. 12, 2016, Rabat.

28. Talea member, interview by the author, Dec. 8, 2016, Rabat.

Even leftist F20 activists who had personal ideological differences with the PJD did not deny the popularity of the PJD in 2011.[29] My interviews revealed that USFP members (a party that competed against the PJD in the 2011 elections) admitted that the PJD win satisfied USFP activists within the F20: "We thought that the winning of the PJD was the start of a new era in Morocco. We thought that this is democracy, at least we have a party, which was really elected, by the people."[30] JCO members tended to simultaneously understand and lament that a PJD win essentially ended the movement. Karim, a prominent JCO activist for more than twenty years, often spoke fondly of leftist F20 activists but, like all JCO members I spoke with, was highly critical of the PJD:

> When Benkirane became the prime minister, that was the beginning of the end of the F20 in the streets. Why? Because Islamists have never had an opportunity to rule in the government. Therefore, using the "card" of Benkirane was not easy [for the regime]. . . . When Benkirane was chosen to be prime minister after the elections, the F20 had two choices: the first choice says there should be no F20 because the demands were achieved. The second choice is to continue protesting. We studied the revolutions in France and Europe. . . . Unfortunately, in the Arab world, people want changes to happen quickly. They had short-term agendas and did not take into account that change occurs through a long-term process. . . . For the average Moroccan, there was a new constitution, reforms, and Benkirane was prime minister, so everything was okay. But for us [the JCO], the Makhzen is the Makhzen. We don't trust that they will change.[31]

Similarly, a JCO leader made it clear that the group was not hopeful in a PJD victory and even suggested that leftists from the USFP would have been better options: "We did not participate in the elections. We boycotted it, and we consider elections were just an instrument to divert anger

29. Talea member from Berkane, interview by the author, Dec. 2, 2016, Rabat.
30. USFP regional leader, interview by the author, Dec. 13, 2016, Agadir.
31. JCO member, interview by the author, Dec. 28, 2016, Casablanca.

and did not answer the calls of the F20. Also, the elections and those who participated in them facilitated the death of the movement, because it [the election] did not answer the demands of the movement. . . . Those that had faith that there would be change [from PJD rule] were surprised and disappointed because of its weak performance, worse than Istiqlal or USFP."[32] A student leader of JCO's youth wing claimed that the JCO does not "draw a line between political parties," since "the real ruler is the king, and the PJD or Independence Party or USFP function in the margin." The same JCO activist claimed that the PJD "used the movement" to win the general election.[33] Despite the animosity against the PJD, JCO members unanimously made clear that a PJD win facilitated the F20's demobilization. A longtime JCO activist from Ain Sebaa, an eastern coastal suburb of Casablanca, lamented that the PJD was the "biggest beneficiaries in the movement."[34] Similarly, a JCO member in Marrakech summed up the common sentiment felt by all F20 activists: "If another party won, the protest would have continued."[35]

A member from another Islamist party, Hizb al-Umma, had a more optimistic view of a PJD victory and believed that the PJD did indeed enjoy the people's support and "thought that we should give Islamists a chance to govern." However, the same activist also thought that "the Makhzen also helped [the PJD win]. It was like a pact between the PJD and the regime: 'You guys [the PJD] quiet down the protests, and we [Makhzen] will give you the government.'"[36]

Independent F20 activists echoed the same sentiment that the state needed the PJD to win in order to quell protests. One independent activist made clear that had the PJD not won the elections, protests would have increased: "Yes, it was a big blow. The regime knew what to do. They knew that if another party other than the PJD won, the movement would

32. JCO leader, interview by the author, Oct. 31, 2016, Rabat.

33. JCO student leader, interview by the author, Oct. 20, 2016, Rabat.

34. JCO member, interview by the author, Nov. 4, 2016, Ain Sebaa.

35. JCO member, interview by the author, Jan. 5, 2017, Marrakech.

36. Hizb al-Umma member, interview by the author, Nov. 5, 2016, Rabat.

have grown. If that would have happened, then the regime would have toppled itself."[37]

Even current MPs believe that a PJD win was in the Makhzen's interest. A CDT MP from the lower house of parliament suggested that the regime let the PJD win in order to demobilize protests and expressed the sentiment that the leftists who initiated the F20 were becoming increasingly frustrated with the PJD:

> They [the PJD] benefited the regime. They saw what was happening in the other countries and said, "So you want change and Islamists," [and the regime said], "Okay, here—take your Islamists" [laughs]. The regime in Morocco is much smarter than others in the region. I mean, Benkirane worked for the regime before. They know who he is. They know the Islamists and where they will end up. It is clear in the past five years that the regime's plan was good. . . . At some point, Benkirane thought that he was loved by everyone, but the Islamists—starting with Khamenei's 1979 revolution in Iran—betray the leftists that supported the revolution, and now in Tunisia and Egypt they might be betrayed at any time. They are not trustworthy. The Islamists are ready to do anything for their organization's benefit, regardless of the others. This is known, and the Islamists work within this framework.[38]

To be clear, there is no evidence of any cooperation between the PJD and the Makhzen to ensure a parliamentary victory during 2011. However, the fact that many interviewees felt that there was covert cooperation between the palace and the PJD suggests a consensus among activists that the regime indeed needed the PJD victory to lessen protests. As discussed, it was the view of many F20 activists that only a PJD victory during the 2011 elections could have ended the F20's protest momentum. Put simply, the palace had a vested interest in a PJD win, even if it did not make it publicly known.

---

37. Independent F20 activist, interview by the author, Feb. 22, 2017, Rabat.
38. CDT MP, interview by the author, Jan. 13, 2017, Rabat.

The Disintegration of the Movement

Following the victory of the PJD, F20 independents along with the JCO—the JCO being the largest component of the F20—left the movement. An F20 cofounder claimed that after the 2011 elections, "there was a split [within the F20]," and "the movement started to fade away."[39] The activists went on to suggest that after the elections, there was a "crisis" within the F20 around whether change would be attempted via voting and no longer in the streets. The split between those individuals that were supportive of the elections and those opposed had a divisive impact on the movement.

On December 18, 2011, just two weeks after election results were announced, the JCO officially withdrew from the F20. According to many activists, this event was the most significant blow to the movement. Some interviewees believed that the JCO left since Islamists were finally in a position of power, while, as we will see, Islamists I interviewed reject this theory. One F20 activist revealed that after the elections, "protests became much smaller"; however, it was the JCO's withdrawal from the movement that devastated its momentum. In his words, "It was like the Left was saying that it is not possible that the JCO would leave the F20."[40] Interviewees suggested that JCO members tended to agree with other independent F20 activists that a PJD victory, although not desired, essentially demobilized the movement. Said differently, continuing protests after the PJD win would have run against the public will. Indeed, most activists did not leave the F20 because they were convinced that the PJD would reform the country. A member of Talea, a leftist component of the F20, expressed that the PJD victory was the main reason F20 protests ended, but he also believed that this abatement of protests by F20 activists was owing to hope on behalf of the Moroccan public and not F20 activists: "The average simple Moroccan thought that this Islamist party [the PJD] would do what the regime's [royalist] parties would not do. So, the regime played the Islamist

39. F20 cofounder, interview by the author, Oct. 1, 2016, Rabat.
40. Independent F20 activist, interview by the author, Feb. 22, 2017, Rabat.

card, and it was the last card it could use. That card gave simple Moroccans hope that it will be a democratic government, and since people voted for Islamists, then we had to allow them to go into the government and work. The PJD had a popular discourse, a discourse that played with the imaginations and minds of Moroccans."[41] This sentiment implies that the public agreed with many F20 activists that the PJD victory was a credible signal that reforms were being implemented. According to an independent activist, both independents and the Islamists were convinced that protests needed to stop after the PJD victory:

> It was clear that there was a big change in the country. It meant that, according to public opinion, there was no need for a social movement like the F20. Therefore, we, the independents of the movement, along with the JCO, had the same exact analysis of the situation, which is that we had to end the movement and try different forms of activism to change the country. . . . The departure of the JCO from the F20 movement was not a surprise. Because they had the same analysis of the situation like us, and we knew that we had to end the movement. The only difference was that we decided to celebrate with champagne [laughs] as a symbolic gesture of saying we fought for one year and enough. . . . For me there is no point to protest just for the sake of protest, without an objective. It was more important for us to fight for democracy, and we couldn't do that within the F20 movement.[42]

Despite the fact that a minority of activists celebrated the PJD victory, most F20 activists believed that the PJD exploited the movement. Many felt that the PJD took advantage of the F20 by using its slogan of "fighting corruption and tyranny" during the 2011 electoral campaign—two of the F20's main contentions with the Makhzen. This sentiment hints at the fact that the PJD promised to fulfill the goals that the F20 initiated. An Islamist F20 member in Rabat elaborated on why some activists felt that the PJD took advantage of the F20: "They [the PJD] stole one of the F20's

41. Talea member, interview by the author, Dec. 8, 2016, Rabat.
42. Independent F20 cofounder, interview by the author, Oct. 26, 2016, Casablanca.

slogans about battling corruption and made it their main slogan in the 2011 elections. If it was not for the F20, there would be no elections. So, they exploited the movement and said to the people that 'we' [the PJD] would fight corruption and tyranny."[43] Even JCO members expressed the same sentiment about the PJD: "The PJD is already in the Makhzen's circle. Before, they never dreamed of being involved in the government, but with the 2011 MENA Uprisings, they could. They benefited from the movement; they were the biggest beneficiaries from the movement."[44]

Following the elections in November, there was a perception that the F20 was composed solely of fringe or extremist groups. Moroccan economist Fouad Abdelmoumni notes that the middle class, especially, became alienated from the F20 after people heard "that part of the movement is made up of Islamist fanatics and fanatical communists."[45] The alienation of the middle class from the F20 was especially damaging, since the F20 was largely a middle-class movement that began attracting lower classes only later on when it went into popular neighborhoods.[46] More important than the F20's class composition, however, was the perception that groups with more revolutionary beliefs were co-opting the movement. In essence, a disconnect between the public and the F20 continued to ensue following the PJD victory of 2011.

Conclusion

An interview with a member of the Constitutional Advisory Committee, which drafted the new Moroccan Constitution, claimed that power sharing with Islamists would be "painful" for the king and that the monarchy

---

43. Hizb al-Umma member, interview by the author, Nov. 5, 2017, Rabat.

44. JCO member, interview by the author, Nov. 4, 2016, Ain Sebaa.

45. "Morocco's Protest Movement Battles on Margins of Arab Spring," Ahram Online, Nov. 23, 2011, https://english.ahram.org.eg/News/27372.aspx.

46. The F20 movement was never a movement largely represented by the upper class, but the middle class was always visible within the movement. F20 figureheads, especially, were often university-educated activists from middle-class families (Rahman 2011). Fakim and Verghese (2014) also note that the F20 was initially a movement of middle-class youth.

"need[ed] to adapt" to the PJD victory.[47] The signal that this scenario
sent to the public is that the king was forced to devolve some of his powers. In times of social unrest, a regime may want to signal a devolution
of power and take real steps toward unprecedented change. The election
of certain opposition parties sends a message to the public that authoritarian leaders are compromising and listening to the public's grievances.
Within Morocco, one of the most contentious grievances leading up to
2011 was the creation and electoral rise of PAM. PAM's founder, Fouad
Ali al-Himma, and the previous Istiqlal prime minister, Abbas el-Fassi,
were symbols of corruption in Morocco and targets of F20 demonstrations. According to my interviews, a win of either of these parties would
have resulted in an increase of protests. A PJD win prior to 2011 would
have been viewed as a threat to the king and the regime. However, following the social unrest of 2011, signaling a devolution of power—via reforms
and the PJD electoral victory—invalidated the need for a social movement
for change.

The PJD victory in the first parliamentary elections since the 2011
MENA Uprisings signaled to the public that real change (reforms) was
occurring. The state needed the PJD to win the 2011 general elections.
Islamists needed to win elections to quell street protests. The PJD victory
substantiated the reforms announced on March 9, while also making the
F20's existence futile. This turn of events, in turn, convinced some F20
activists to stop protesting, while also changing bystanders' perceptions
about the necessity of continuing F20 protests. In essence, the unprecedented Islamist victory convinced activists that the movement needed to
end. Even JCO members, who are historical rivals with the PJD, admitted
that after the elections, the movement "exhausted its purpose."[48] Moreover, the JCO withdrawal from the streets essentially marked the end of
all major F20 protests. Activists recognized that the continuance of F20
protests following the PJD surprise victory would have run contrary to the

47. "Al-Tuzi: It Is Very Painful for the King to Accept the Sharing of Power with the
Islamists," *Hespress*, Dec. 5, 2011, https://www.hespress.com/interviews/42687.html.

48. JCO leader, interview by the author, Oct. 31, 2016, Rabat.

will of the Moroccan public. A broad implication of this chapter is that not manipulating elections may lessen protests. Said differently, the election of some opposition parties can serve the interests of regimes and demobilize ongoing protests. This chapter fills an important gap in the authoritarian elections literature by showing how authoritarian regimes can use election results to demobilize social movements, and ultimately prolong their rule.

Finally, the 2011 elections had divisive effects within the movement. The election results demonstrated to many that the movement's demands were met; however, the elections worked against the F20. While some activists were supportive of the election results, others were not, and this divide caused some activists to leave the F20. Members of the F20 who supported the election results found themselves shunned or accused of working with the Makhzen: "We were attacked as being part of the state, we were accused of being Makhzen, just because we said we should not attack Benkirane in that moment, because he didn't do anything yet. [I thought,] 'Let's give him time.' Attacking him would be attacking the people's choice."[49] In other words, some activists who were satisfied with the election results believed that they ought to respect the people's will, even if they did not identify ideologically with the Islamist framework of the PJD. This popular belief caused further divisions within the F20 with revolutionary activists accusing fellow F20 reformist members of being co-opted by the regime. The next chapter will cover this divide between "reformists" and "revolutionaries" in detail.

49. F20 activist, interview by the author, Sept. 22, 2016, Mohammedia.

5

Internal Fracture

Structure, Coalitions, and the Tactical Standstill of the F20

One of the problems with the F20 is its leaderless structure. It's a strength and a weakness.

—F20 activist

The F20's horizontally organized nature fostered an Islamist-Marxist coalition, which exacerbated internal conflicts between some leftists and Islamists and ultimately led to the F20's tactical standstill. In other words, rather than hold an array of different protest tactics, the F20 held predictable weekly protests in public spaces.[1] The consequences of this tactical standstill were that the F20 failed to attract attention and supporters to their cause, especially since their initial demands were met through the king's reforms.

The F20 was not a movement solely composed of independent activists; rather, most F20 activists were members of political parties. Political parties directed their followers about when and where to protest. As previously discussed, the JCO was the main source of protesters within the F20, which was, in the words of one activist, "as organized as an army."[2] The JCO was the most hierarchically organized group in the F20—as JCO activists obeyed decisions made directly by their leader. At the time, the

---

1. In Rabat protests would typically occur in front of parliament every Sunday for three to four hours.

2. F20 activist, interview by the author, Oct. 26, 2016, Casablanca.

JCO was led by its founder, Sheikh Abdessalam Yassine. Internal intolerance to Yassine was not tolerated, but since his death in 2012, the JCO has been more internally democratic. The JCO is still highly hierarchical with the higher council (now two people) making final decisions (like whether to protest) (Sakthivel 2014).

The effectiveness of the JCO is most visible in their leader's ability to mobilize tens of thousands of its adherents to the street and, in turn, remove them from the streets.[3] As we will see, the JCO was able to exploit the F20's structureless nature in order to increase the JCO's influence and control of the movement.[4] The JCO accomplished this feat by allying with influential leftists (the DWP) and becoming more influential within the F20. Specifically, I contend that the F20's structure and ideologically diverse composition facilitated both internal co-optation of the F20 by the JCO and an inability of the movement to change its tactics beyond predictable weekly protests. As we will see, these factors generated internal conflicts and led to the eventual withdrawal of the JCO from the F20. According to JCO members I interviewed, the main reasons for their withdrawal from the F20 were that the F20 was no longer effective and that the JCO was repeatedly targeted and attacked by some leftists within the F20. Regardless of the reasons, F20 protests immediately declined with the withdrawal of the JCO.

As discussed throughout this book, ideological heterogeneity was a defining feature of the F20, and a shared identity among F20 activists was lacking. According to Thierry Desrues, "ideological incompatibility" between leftist and Islamist activists may explain why the F20 never had official leaders or figureheads (2013, 415). This lack of official leadership within the F20 has had various consequences for the movement. The F20 is an example of what Zeynep Tufekci calls networked and horizontalist social movements. This social movement composition denotes the leaderless and structureless nature of movements, which are usually products

3. Hierarchy is the "right that some have to oblige others to comply with central decisions" (Ahrne and Brunsson 2011, 86).

4. The F20 is not a vertically organized group with clear membership numbers and leaders. I use the term *structureless* to refer to a lack of formal leadership structures.

of online activism. Tufekci correctly notes how modern movements use "digital tools to rapidly amass large numbers protesters with a common goal," but owing to a lack of "leadership structures" and "collective decision-making capabilities," the movement will likely falter (2017, xxiii). Said differently, structureless movements, like the F20, are often more susceptible to internal movement fracture.

The F20's lack of leadership structures facilitated the movement's tactical rigidity. A prime example of tactical innovation (as opposed to rigidity) can be seen during the US civil rights movement where a combination of marches, sit-ins, economic boycotts, and blockages pressured the US government to change policies. This variance in tactics was not the case for the F20. A core finding of social movement studies is that "activists who are able to adopt new tactics in the face of their opponents' responses are also more likely to experience protest success" (Wang and Soule 2016, 518). By November 2011, the F20's predictable weekly protests in public spaces could not adequately respond to the regime's varied campaign of concessions and repression. Public spaces refer to traditional areas for protest activity. For example, in Rabat protests would be in front of the parliament. Conflicts concerning whether to move protests beyond public spaces and to popular neighborhoods essentially led to the tactical rigidity that would characterize the F20. Popular neighborhoods are lower-income and densely populated suburbs of large cities. In the words of a USP member in Tangier: "The F20 did not try to develop new methods—it became boring for people—every week we would meet on Sunday and go to a march for three to four hours. Therefore, citizens saw that the same thing happened every week, and they started to get bored [with the F20]."[5]

As we will see, the F20 was able to initially unite different political organizations by ignoring ideological differences between leftists and Islamists. However, a contentious JCO-DWP alliance not only gave rise to more ideological conflicts within the movement, but also allowed the JCO to be more influential within the F20. The JCO-DWP coalition attempted to move protests into popular neighborhoods, which increased internal

---

5. USP member, interview by the author, Feb. 25, 2017, Tangier.

conflicts within the F20. In essence, the F20's structure facilitated internal conflicts and led to the JCO's withdrawal from the F20 and the subsequent end to all major F20 protests.

The Movement's "Structure"

The F20 is not a vertically organized group with clear membership numbers and leaders, but the movement attempted to establish more united collective decision-making structures. A core group of activists, often referred to in French as the Noyau du (Hard Core), was formed in the early days of movement and acted as a small advising committee that proposed times and places for demonstrations to be held. Protesters were not "members" but an amalgamation of various young individuals convinced by the F20's simple message of "Freedom, Dignity, and Social Justice." One independent activist made this point clear: "I don't say that I am a February 20 [member]—I am [name omitted]. The February 20 Movement is made up of individuals. It is a movement for different groups to achieve a common goal."[6] Following the initial call to protest, political parties and elite figureheads began assisting the movement, eventually becoming integral to the F20.[7] Political parties and organizations were central to the F20's committees. These committees are known as Tansaqiat in Morocco and were created at the beginning of the movement in February 2011.

More than twenty organizations supported the F20, but the main participants can be seen in figure 2. Decision making within the F20 was inspired by the participatory democracy model and a rejection of formal leaders.[8] Very much like the Occupy Wall Street movement, the F20 had "general assemblies" that occurred in Rabat or Casablanca. The first general assembly was held in USP offices in Casablanca. Within general assemblies, which were open to the public, activists would vote on proposals, usually concerning where and when to protest, along with demands. These assemblies attracted hundreds of participants, each of whom could

6. F20 independent, interview by the author, Sept. 19, 2016, Casablanca.
7. F20 Majlis Dahm leader, interview by the author, Feb. 21, 2017, Rabat.
8. Participatory democracy implies making decisions based on a general consensus without formal leaders.

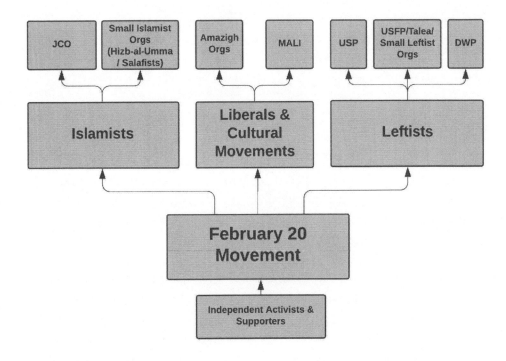

speak for an unlimited amount of time. Some tasks were delegated to groups of activists within committees. The decisions within the national assembly would, usually, spread to local committees (*tansaqiat mahalia*) that existed in each city where the F20 was active. Within F20 general assemblies, activists could vote on measures concerning where and when to protest. Local committees, however, had no power other than organizing F20 members together for discussions. One activist noted, "In general, the demands in Rabat would spread to other local committees" and that the F20's organizational "ambiguity" led to a movement that was not united on basic decisions, like when to protest.[9]

The Media Committee would set up interviews with news outlets and help create propaganda videos, while the Support Committee would

9. Amazigh activist, interview by the author, Oct. 4, 2016, Rabat.

attempt to secure funding for the movement. However, interviewees often expressed that committees were chaotic and had few decision-making capabilities.[10] This situation was in large part owing to the fact that political organizations (like the JCO and USP) had their own leaders and decision makers who would direct their members (that is, when and where to protest). Other F20 activists felt that these committees were just extensions of political parties. For instance, one independent activist claimed that the F20 Support Committee (Majlis Dahm) "was an extension of a party" since the founder was a member of the USP.[11] In essence, the formation of different committees would often be dominated by political organizations. This feature caused conflicts with independents and smaller parties that felt their voices were being drowned out by political parties and other organizations.

Ahmed Benchemsi believes that the leaderless structure of the F20 was "a guarantee of its inclusivity because it allowed large numbers of people with different opinions and ideologies to coexist in the same environment without having to compete for control." Benchemsi also recognizes that "not electing representatives condemned F20 to strategic paralysis, since no one could make decisions in the movement's name and no clear group decision could be made by the unwieldy general assemblies" (2014, 219). Various social movement theorists have claimed that unofficial leaders come out of leaderless movements. Den Hond, Bakker, and Smith note, even in antihierarchical social movements, "stratification of power within a movement is likely to occur" (2015, 297). Jo Freeman (1972) makes a similar observation about the 1960s women's liberation movement. She concludes that there is no such thing as structureless movements, since informal leaders rise to power within movements. Yet even within leaderless movements, "hierarchy and power reappear" (Benkler 2013, 216). This implies that even for horizontalist movements, like the F20, certain

10. Ahmed Benchemsi notes that during the "chaotic" general assemblies, "everyone spoke in turn without a time limit" and that "this system was unable to produce any agenda" (2014, 219–20).

11. F20 independent, interview by the author, Feb. 22, 2017, Rabat.

groups will be more powerful than others and have more control of the movement.

Mohamad Masbah (2015), a researcher at the Carnegie Middle East Center, notes that the F20's lack of structure ended the movement because members were unable to manage differences among themselves (Mesbah 2015). Abdelaziz Radi similarly suggests that "the lack of stable, coherent and strong leadership made it permeable to any tactical infiltration" (2017, 53). Radi essentially claims that the F20's lack of unity exposed it to targeted online smearing. The regime was able to screen the F20's online activity and knew how to attack the movement's weaknesses by exploiting preexisting divides among participants (that is, Islamists and secular leftists). The regime was able to disseminate propaganda concerning contentious issues that leftists and Islamists disagreed on, and without a leadership structure, the F20 could not mediate conflicts concerning such issues. What Radi and Masbah suggest is that leadership and a hierarchical movement structure are needed to successfully manage such an ideologically diverse social movement. As we will see, this same lack of structure led to the F20's tactical rigidity, internal co-optation, and eventually the withdrawal of the JCO.

F20's Initial Tactic: Brushing Ideology under the Rug

> In the beginning it was a very beautiful experience, especially in relation to the [political] organizations. They turned a blind eye to the ideological differences.[12]
> —Leftist F20 activist

During the initial months of protests and F20 committee gatherings, Islamists and leftists learned more about one another. In the words of one Islamist activist: "The F20 movement was an opportunity to meet and get to know some of the leftists."[13] Another JCO activist illustrates how preconceptions and stereotypes about opposing ideological groups were

12. CDT Union MP, interview by the author, Jan. 13, 2017, Rabat.
13. JCO student, interview by the author, Oct. 20, 2016, Rabat.

broken when leftists and Islamist worked together during the inception of the F20:

> Leftists used to think that Islamists were terrorists. That we oppress and hit our wives, that we don't give women their rights. When we got closer [with leftists], we became very surprised. I remember . . . it was my wife's birthday, and I told them that today is a special day, and I will not be present to attend a meeting, and some leftists were surprised that I celebrate my wife's birthday. I told them, on the contrary, if you practice true political Islam, then women's rights will be more protected than within progressive leftism. We are not Salafists, which means we are not extreme.[14]

Committee meetings, according to interviewees, were completely open to the public (including antimovement spies), and members expressed an array of opinions in an unstructured manner (which covered various issues at once), while only logistical decisions were made. The cooperative and chaotic space that the F20 provided was also where the battle over the F20's identity took place. For instance, whether to hold protests on religious holidays and allow the use religious slogans and banners, like Islamic slogans in solidarity with Syrian protesters, were among the disagreements that eventually arose within the F20.[15] There were also disagreements over how best to convince the public of the movement's legitimacy. Islamists viewed religious symbolism (public prayers during protests, religious chants, and gender segregation) as culturally resonant to the Moroccan public. Leftists often viewed religious symbols as strategic threats to potential recruits, especially considering the violent outcomes that Islamists were blamed for in Syria and Iraq. These pragmatic reasons concerning the Islamic presence within the F20 eventually turned into ethical discussions about participating in a movement with a group that many leftists felt were their ideological enemies.

14. JCO member, interview by the author, Dec. 28, 2016, Casablanca.
15. Hizb al-Umma member, interview by the author, Nov. 5, 2016, Rabat.

Initially, ideology was put aside so that a broad coalition of groups could work under the umbrella of the F20. There was a consensus that previous ideological enemies needed each other to hold large demonstrations and ultimately pressure the regime for change. However, this broad coalition came at the expense of ignoring ideological cleavages and delaying discussions about various issues like freedom of religion, gender equality, and LGBT rights, among other things. The structure of the F20 facilitated the mobilization of movement since it was a movement open to all. It allowed the movement to quickly organize a diverse array of activists. Despite early success, as Zeynep Tufekci (2017) emphasizes, without a clear and united strategy, maintaining the movement would be substantially more difficult. The lack of a united decision-making body within the F20 led to a movement that was free to have an array of diverse slogans and messages. Revolutionaries and reformists worked within the same movement but had divergent demands. As demonstrated by Benford and Snow (2000), a movement needs a united frame and message to be successful, which the F20 lacked. A JCO leader noted that the F20 was successful in mobilizing masses owing to an initial strategy of "delaying" discussions that would highlight ideological differences:

> The points of difference were initially clear. In practice, we tried not to highlight these strong divides and work toward the goal that the F20 decided on, which is focused on democracy, human rights, and change in the political system. These are ideas that generally had differing views initially. It is true that there were many differences, but at the beginning we decided to delay these discussions until a later stage, because if we would have discussed these things in the early stages of the movement, it would have threatened the movement and ended it in the beginning. It [the movement] needed the power of many groups so that it would have the power to pressure the political system and achieve the demanded changes.[16]

Therefore, the JCO, an organization that is clear about its ambitions of establishing an Islamic state without a monarch, "withdrew principles"

16. JCO leader, interview by the author, Oct. 31, 2016, Rabat.

and was "very tolerant of all sides" so that the F20 movement could be successful in pressuring the state.[17] The JCO strategically ignored ideological contradictions within the F20. According to many leftists and independents I interviewed, the JCO made many "concessions" to other leftist organizations and independents: "During Ramadan [July–August 2011] we had meetings, and the JCO would stay with us [in the meetings]. They are extremists and very religious, and they were not bothered when we ate, drank, and smoked in front of them during Ramadan, even though this contradicts their rules and ideological beliefs."[18] This restraint was even evident within the committees of the F20: "They [the JCO] went to the committees, but not in large numbers. They wanted to avoid conflict within the F20. . . . Their numbers were in the streets."[19] The JCO was restrained even regarding "Ramadan eat-ins" staged by the pro-personal-liberties organization MALI. In 2009, MALI organized a protest against a law criminalizing public eating during Ramadan by staging a public eat-in at the train station in Mohammedia, a port city between Casablanca and Rabat. They continued to stage eat-ins within the F20 during the month of Ramadan (July–August 2011). JCO members were restrained when the eat-ins occurred and did not attack MALI members. The same was true for LGBT activists as well: "In regard to Islamists, there was an actual respect between them and others. Homosexuals were in the movement too. They were few, and no one attacked them or rejected them, even the Islamists."[20]

Similar to the JCO, MALI members initially avoided discussions important to them, like issues pertaining to personal liberties and gender equality, in February 2011. In the words of one MALI activist, "In the beginning, we did not want to discuss things that could divide the movement. We focused on the things that gathered people and not the things that divide."[21] Nonetheless, issues concerning gender equality and what

17. JCO leader, interview by the author, Oct. 31, 2016, Rabat.

18. Talea member, interview by the author, Dec. 8, 2016, Rabat.

19. Journalist F20 participant, interview by the author, Jan. 12, 2017, Rabat.

20. AMDH leader, interview by the author, Nov. 30, 2016, Rabat.

21. MALI member, interview by the author, Mar. 13, 2017, Rabat.

some perceived as direct provocations of Islamists within the F20 started in March, yet the JCO seemed to make concessions by joining protests that called for gender equality.[22] The strategic decision by organizations, like MALI and the JCO, to delay discussions concerning ideology, focusing instead on broad and reformist demands, resulted in the movement being able to attract the support of previously apolitical members of society. Mekouar notes that during the first "ascending phase" of the F20 (roughly February to April 2011), "normal people" were visible in the movement along with political organizations (2016, 102). Before conflicts concerning framing, and subsequently ideology, began to pervade F20 discussions in March 2011, JCO members were granted full "membership" within the F20, which meant the group participated in planning and coordinating protests. The key to maintaining the fragile cooperation between competing ideological groups was avoiding discussion about the details of each group's view of what "a democratic state" should be:

> I remember on Friday, February 19th, in the first time in my life, I entered the offices of the USP in Casablanca. I and others from the JCO went in their offices, and we were surprised that we were with other youth that did not have the same political or cultural or ideological ideas, but we all agreed that Morocco should become a democratic state. "What is democracy, and how we should understand it?" It was not the time and place to discuss that; rather, it was the time and place to prepare how we would go out to the streets [to protest].[23]

Therefore, although leftists and Islamists united around broad demands of democracy, specific discussion about what a democratic state is was initially avoided, and such issues would eventually be contentiously discussed within the F20. Despite initial restraint on behalf of the JCO, ideological conflict became an increasing problem for the F20 following the announcement of reforms by the king in March 2011. This conflict was deepened after a contentious alliance between the JCO and the DWP

22. F20 independent, interview by the author, Oct. 26, 2016, Rabat.
23. JCO member, interview by the author, Dec. 28, 2016, Casablanca.

formed. Said differently, brushing contentious topics "under the rug" could last only so long. Conversations about political demands became ideologically based divisions. At that point, various leftists, especially the USP, began to attack the JCO and accuse the organization of being incompatible with the democratic ideals of the F20. However, the increasingly ideologically based contentions were facilitated by the F20's open and horizontal structure. The F20's lack of structure essentially allowed one movement to employ divergent tactics with divergent methods. The next section will demonstrate how the F20's structure facilitated internal cooptation by the JCO and how the movement eventually became dependent on the foot power of the JCO. In essence, the next section outlines how "hierarchy and power reappear" within horizontalist and structureless movements (Benkler 2013, 216).

Contentious Alliances and the Formation of Factions within the F20

Following the referendum campaign and general elections, the F20 began to lose public support and became dependent on the JCO for its survival. Indeed, some estimate that the JCO composed 50 to 60 percent of demonstrators in big cities and around 90 percent in small ones (Mekouar 2015, 99). However, although the JCO was the largest organization in the movement, it lacked internal legitimacy within the F20.[24] The lack of internal legitimacy implied that groups and independents within the F20 respected and worked with the DWP, the JCO's new ally, but not with the JCO. This fact was clear during interviews where leftists often referred to DWP members as "brothers" and allies, while Islamists were described as incompatible with the F20's democratic and secular ideals. According to activists, the JCO, which is perceived by most F20 members as an extremist Islamist organization, should not represent or lead the movement. The JCO's decision to ally itself with one of the smallest and more

---

24. The JCO has anywhere from two to five hundred thousand members and is the largest and most organized nongovernmental political organization in the country (Sakthivel 2014).

radical Marxist organizations, the DWP, may seem baffling prima facie. However, the DWP did have the internal legitimacy that the JCO lacked among leftists within the F20. Moreover, the DWP's close ties with the Moroccan Association of Human Rights makes the JCO-DWP coalition more logical. Indeed, all members of AMDH I interviewed were also DWP members. The AMDH is the largest and most influential human rights organization in Morocco and an organization that played a pivotal role in popularizing the F20. The AMDH provided not only space for meetings in their offices and filming equipment for F20 propaganda videos, but also the support of widely respected human rights activists who were leaders or members of the AMDH. Although leaders and figureheads of the AMDH tend to be DWP members, some members of the human rights organization were Islamists, independents, Amazigh activists, and other leftist parties. Furthermore, the AMDH served as a broker between different ideological currents.[25] Figure 3 illustrates that as a broker that connected various groups, the AMDH was an asset to a JCO-DWP coalition mainly owing to the close ties between the AMDH and the DWP. Again, the AMDH and the DWP are often viewed as united organizations, the main distinction being that the AMDH is a human rights organization, whereas the DWP is a political party.

As shown in figure 3, an alliance with the DWP is essentially an alliance with the AMDH, which was an easy way for the JCO to gain influential allies and, more important, increase control within the F20. The AMDH was the only organization that had experience connecting Islamists and leftist activists together. For instance, the F20's coordination-committee structure was created initially by the AMDH in 2008 to link various leftists in committees that would combat the high cost of living (Monjib 2011; Benchemsi 2014). The F20 adopted this same structure to link different activists together in 2011. Bennani-Chraïbi and Jeghllaly note the

---

25. Tarrow and Tilly's (2003) concept of brokerage, that is, the production of a new connection between previously unconnected or weakly connected social sites in relation to the spread of mobilizations, can help us better conceive how the political phenomena of revolutions, protests, and social movements disseminate.

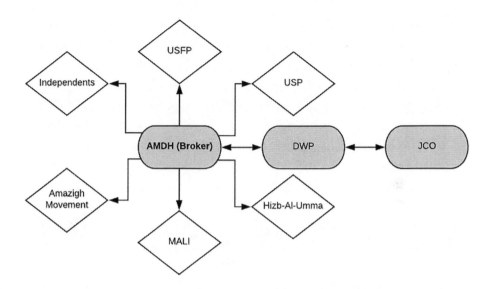

central role that the AMDH played in the F20: "From the beginning, the AMDH's support was crucial. Drawing on its pioneering role at the heart of multiple networks, the AMDH acted as both a transmission channel and a reservoir of human resources and logistical know-how. Moreover, it contributed to the socialization and generational renewal of the radical left" (2012, 114). After the JCO-DWP alliance formed, Islamists became more influential within the F20 and the ad hoc coordination committees. One Amazigh activist from the Rif region felt that Islamist control of the F20 led the movement to ignore formally addressing important issues like personal liberties (LGBT) rights: "When I wrote [an online blog] about the topic of individual rights, it was discussed in the local committees, in Rabat and other cities, but the JCO did not [discuss it]. So, they [the F20] refused! They refused to discuss it. This shows that the group that won was the Islamists."[26] The highly organized JCO was easily able to influence the movement and attempted to control the F20's objectives and tactics. The increasingly religious and more revolutionary tone of F20 protests was

26. Amazigh activist, interview by the author, Oct. 4, 2016, Rabat.

owing to the JCO-DWP stance on raising the "ceiling of demands." Similarly, the JCO and the DWP were united in attempting to move protests into some popular neighborhoods. This alliance is why an independent activist felt that the JCO's dominance of the logistics committee[27] was especially damaging to the movement: "The danger with them [the JCO] is that they were part of the logistics committee, so it was them that organized the protests, that had the cars and loudspeakers; they [the JCO] had the heart of the movement. The failure is that the movement has been clear that it is loosely organized."[28] The same activist explains that the JCO's influence within the general assembly and its decision to go into some popular neighborhoods were the last straw for many leftists, especially moderates and those individuals from the middle classes: "After the general assembly of the F20 concluded to take the protests from downtowns [public spaces] to the popular neighborhoods in the outskirts of the city, it was noticed that many components withdrew from the movement owing to the domination of the JCO [within the general assembly]. . . . So many people, especially those that belonged to the middle class, refused this [JCO] domination and left the movement, and when days passed the presence of activists became very weak."[29] Leftist activists also felt that the JCO began influencing the "Hard Core" (Noyau du) group of F20 figureheads. This perception led to an intercommittee divide:[30] "The JCO entered [controlled F20 committees] and divided [the F20]. They created a new divide within the F20. One side was with the Noyau du [Hard Core committee of figureheads], and the other was against the Noyau du."[31] Although the "Hard Core" had little decision-making power, the perception by leftists that Islamists were co-opting and taking over this important (initially

27. This committee has been described as the "heart of the movement" in some cities. See "The Moroccan 'February 20' Movement: Young People Revolt, Islamists Rule," *Bidayat Magazine*, accessed Apr. 20, 2017, https://bidayatmag.com/node/290.

28. F20 independent, interview by the author, Sept. 22, 2016, Mohammedia.

29. F20 independent, interview by the author, Sept. 19, 2016, Casablanca.

30. This fracture refers to a divide between different committees (that is, logistics committee versus support committee).

31. F20 independent, interview by the author, Sept. 19, 2016, Casablanca.

leftist) committee had a real impact on internal conflicts and divides. Kleber Ghimire notes that within social movements, "actors may not only be able to attain important organizational power, but also possess the capacity to plainly justify their legitimacy through diverse means even when their actions are contradictory or designed primarily to suit their narrow interests" (2011, 7). The JCO attempted to attain increased influence within the F20 through an alliance with the DWP. Therefore, the JCO's alliance with the DWP may seem contradictory since these two groups have competing ideologies, but this alliance was instrumental in allowing the JCO to increase its power within the movement. The open structure of the F20 essentially allowed the movement to be internally co-opted, which implies that some organizations began increasing their influence within the F20 committees. Said differently, the JCO's alliance with the DWP, which happens to be the most influential group within the AMDH (the largest human rights organization within Morocco), is no coincidence. In the words of one independent, the JCO started an "internal insurgency" and elaborates on why this alliance occurs: "The DWP is the smallest party by numbers in Morocco. They have no power in the streets. They can't have a protest in Rabat with more than fifty people. Therefore, the JCO has the numbers. The DWP wanted to take advantage of the JCO, and the JCO wanted to have an ally within the F20. The JCO could not stay isolated among three leftist parties. Those were the [mutually beneficial] interests that they each had in each other."[32]

My interviews revealed that political conflicts concerning the F20's demands[33] eventually turned into ideologically based conflicts "when the DWP started coordinating with the JCO." Some leftists believed that the JCO-DWP agreement to no longer limit the F20's demands to reforms was a blow against the secular and democratic goals of other leftists."[34] According to JCO members, their alliance with the DWP functioned because both parties have similar goals of establishing a state without a

32. Independent F20 activist, interview by the author, Feb. 22, 2017, Rabat.
33. This divide implies conflicts concerning *Saqf al-mutalib* covered in chapter 2 and refers to discussions concerning the type of regime the F20 should demand.
34. Independent F20 activist, interview by the author, Feb. 22, 2017, Rabat.

monarch. In the words of one JCO member, "Their [the DWP's] goals for a state are similar to the society and political system that the JCO wants."[35] Therefore, the JCO and the DWP agreed on important stances, like going into popular neighborhoods and taking a more revolutionary tone in slogans. Other leftists were highly skeptical of the alliance, since Islamists, and especially the JCO's interpretation of Islamism, were incompatible with the democratic ideals of leftists. A member of Talea who attended various F20 meetings in Rabat and Casablanca believed that ideologically based conflicts were largely overlooked within the F20 until the JCO began working with the DWP: "In the beginning of the movement, the ideological differences were not clear and not very big. It was buried and not evident. After a period of time there was unification between the JCO, a group that is Islamist, extremist, with extreme ideas, and that does not believe in a democratic state, but an Islamic state, and the DWP. This weird alliance was evident during an F20 meeting. Since this meeting the ideological differences within the F20 started."[36] Other independent leftists thought that the JCO's and the DWP's proposition to keep the ceiling of demands open and let people decide on the type of state they wanted was "too democratic," especially since Moroccans tend to support the king. A former journalist who was very active within the F20 revealed that letting the people decide on what type of state the F20 should demand was not prudent, since most Moroccans would opt for a monarchy: "The JCO and the DWP wanted to let the choice [of what government type to demand] to be open to the people, but Moroccans are not educated enough to have a democratic choice. They need some leaders to show them the road. If people want a country with a king, then what are they going to say? The majority of Moroccans say that the government does nothing, and the king does everything. So, if you leave the choice to the people, we are going to have a disaster."[37] Some members questioned the policies that the JCO and the DWP wanted to impose on the F20, while others raised

35. JCO leader, interview by the author, Oct. 31, 2016, Rabat.
36. Talea member, interview by the author, Dec. 8, 2016, Rabat.
37. Ex-journalist, interview by the author, Jan. 19, 2017, Rabat.

concerns about how decisions were being made within the general assemblies. For example, leftist interviewees lamented that some F20 protests were divided by gender and that increased religious slogans and symbols were visible within the movement.[38] Others decried that the JCO imposed more revolutionary goals on the F20. Still other leftists expressed that they could not directly address specific ideological issues with the JCO:

> In a general assembly there are two to three hundred participants, and we make decisions with votes, and they [the JCO and DWP] are the majority. We [independent leftists] were sixty to seventy people. They were two hundred. So, they made decisions on things before they came and voted. Therefore, we began speaking with them about what is democracy. Is democracy the right to vote or not? So here we started discussing democracy and values, and when we started to talk about these things, they got very angry, very angry. To the point where they verbally attacked [us], and they decided to stop communicating with us.[39]

The fact that the JCO and the DWP dominated general assemblies is clear. However, when independent leftists questioned how decisions were being made within these assemblies, JCO members stopped communicating with them altogether. Leftists from the USP, Talea, and independents started questioning the presence of the JCO within the F20 and considered banning the JCO from F20 meetings. The figurehead of the influential Support Committee of the F20 revealed that, in the view of the committee and the USP, the JCO-DWP coalition "inflated" the regime's propaganda that the F20 was composed only of radicals and that this issue weakened the movement.[40] Other leftists had a less pragmatic view of the Marxist-Islamist alliance and felt that their leftist allies betrayed them for Islamists.[41] Most leftist interviewees, however, agreed that the JCO was essentially using the F20 for its political agenda and saw the alliance

38. USFP member, interview by the author, Nov. 24, 2016, Casablanca.
39. F20 independent, interview by the author, Sept. 22, 2016, Mohammedia.
40. Majlis Dahm leader, interview by the author, Feb. 21, 2017, Rabat.
41. F20 communist-independent, interview by the author, Dec. 12, 2016, Agadir.

with the DWP as facilitating that goal. Interestingly, JCO members felt that the USP was using the F20 for its own purposes and "took advantage of the movement for its own goals" to further its "political agenda."[42] These conflicts not only divided the F20's stances on issues but also affected the group's ability to organize protests in response to the regime's coordinated campaign of concessions and repression.

The F20's Divided Strategy and Fracture

McCammon and Moon find that diverse coalitions are more likely to endure "when they acknowledge threats to cooperation and resolve internal conflicts" and develop a joint identity (2015, 334). Furthermore, Jones et al. (2001) find that coalitions are more effective at mobilizing people when a united movement "leads the planning and decision making while drawing on other organizations to assist" (McCammon and Moon 2010, 332). These findings have important implications for the F20. The committees within the F20 were created to make decisions about funding, planning protest events, and banners and slogans. However, the F20 lacked a joint identity and message, and many leftists believed that the movement and these committee were overrun by Islamists.[43] Essentially, the F20 failed to develop the key elements of a united strategy. The movement could not resolve internal conflicts or develop a united identity precisely because the F20 did not have a united decision-making apparatus. As such, the movement could not move beyond their most predictable tactic of holding weekly protests and marches. This situation was detrimental for the F20 because movements need to have a variety of protest tactics to both attract attention to their grievances and gain more protesters (McAdam 1983). In the case of the F20, the king's unprecedented reforms took attention away from the movement and made the F20's existence appear increasingly unnecessary. As we will see in the next section, an influential political organization within the F20, the JCO, effectively exploited the F20's structureless nature. Independents and less influential parties used to control

42. JCO student leader, interview by the author, Oct. 20, 2016, Rabat.
43. This perception was in large part owing to the smear campaign.

general assemblies, but this situation changed when the JCO co-opted them and attempted to alter the movement's strategy and tactics.

Internal JCO Co-optation

Independent activists were responsible for bringing the F20 movement to life. The first calls to protest were from independent activists, and F20 committees were initially well represented by independents. Influential political parties eventually dominated committees and general assemblies that F20 independents helped create. Kleber Ghimire's study of the loosely organized, transnational Alternative Globalization Movement finds that the "blurry hierarchal structure and decision-making procedure made internal decision-making 'precarious.'" Ghimire raises the question about who has the right to speak for loosely organized movements and why. Asked differently, "Where did the political legitimacy come from for exercising important organizational power" (2011, 107)? As Ghimire observes, the question of who speaks for a movement is important, since even loosely organized movements need to have a unified message and strategy to resonate with bystanders, which structureless movements often lack.

F20 members expressed frustration with the informal hierarchies forming within the horizontally organized movement. During the first months of the movement, the F20's first movers were recognized figureheads. "First movers" refers to the few individual activists who called for protest under the banner of the F20. These figureheads were not deliberately selected through some internal decision-making process (that is, elections). Instead, they became the face of the movement because of their charisma and visibility in the media. These figureheads, however, had no extraordinary legitimacy and no power over the decision-making processes within the F20.

Well-organized groups did overcome the horizontal structure of the F20 and created informal hierarchies, especially within the decision-making process. These informal hierarchies helped split the movement. Independent F20 members expressed frustration with the influence that political organizations like the JCO and the DWP had on committees. Independent members were also concerned that logistical decisions concerning the time and place of protests were predetermined prior to the

F20 general assembly meetings.[44] Similarly, Amazigh activists felt that they had little influence and presence within the F20 committees.[45] USFP members from the F20 also complained that decisions were increasingly being made "behind the curtains" and that the general assembly was "symbolic" because decisions were already made.[46] This sentiment was especially pervasive among independents and less influential parties. In the words of one Hizb al-Umma member in Rabat: "Afterward the groups got together and tried to control the movement, and here is where the conflicts and clashes began about how to build up this movement."[47] One independent F20 activist became disillusioned with the decision-making process within the F20 and decided to no longer attend meetings he found to be, in his words, pointless: "I understood that in the meetings, people would just decide on when they would go and protest. So, what's the point? People are making decisions outside of the meetings, so why are we losing time fighting?"[48] Another independent F20 activist spoke to me about being in an F20 general assembly, and his story sheds light on just how much power politically affiliated members of the F20 had within the movement:

> One day, I confronted an activist [within a F20 general assembly] because he came to the meetings to just reiterate what his party already decided on. I asked him why. He said that I am in a party, and the party made this decision. [He asked,] "Do you think that I would go to the [F20] meetings and say something that contradicts my party?" I understood that this was natural, but this was one of the problems. The biggest problem was that the youth of the JCO were 100 percent controlled by their organization, and other party members were too. This does not

44. F20 independent and ex-TV journalist, interview by the author, Jan. 17, 2019, Rabat.

45. Amazigh movement leader, interview by the author, Dec. 8, 2016, Rabat.

46. USFP leader, interview by the author, Nov. 24, 2016, Casablanca.

47. Two Hizb al-Umma members, interview by the author, Nov. 5, 2016, Rabat.

48. Independent F20 activist, interview by the author, Jan. 19, 2017, Rabat.

mean that all of the youth were part of a party. On the contrary, there were perhaps more independents [than people affiliated with parties] in the movement. However, when there is an independent individual that is not affiliated with a party, he will be attacked by other political groups. Like what happened to [name omitted of F20 independent].[49]

Benchemsi claims that the F20 lacked a "unified and consistent strategy to counter the Makhzen" and that it was because of a lack of structure and "decision making process" (2014, 225). Benchemsi concludes that "the haphazard nature" of the F20 led to its collapse and that a lack of structure and leadership led the F20 "to be hijacked by their most radical members" (226). More important, decisions within general assembly meetings never moved beyond "let's demonstrate" (219). Regardless of how much power these committees had, the perception that political parties were hijacking the movement was a common sentiment. For example, another independent F20 activist elaborated on how he believed that the JCO and AMDH used certain committees to control the movement: "A problem was that some people made decisions outside of the F20, like some people in the AMDH and JCO let youth play in the rooms [general assemblies] but made decisions for them. That was one of the big problems. They created what we called the Support Committee of F20. That was a big disaster. There was no support, really. They just tried to influence the youth, and they tried to make decisions for them."[50] In essence, the F20 was a movement that was founded by independent activists; however, the presence of organized political organizations drowned out the voices of less organized independent activists, along with less influential parties. Many interviewees felt that the JCO, along with other more revolutionary elements like the DWP, became more dominant within the F20 by exploiting the movement's horizontal structure. The lack of unification within meetings also led to a tactical standstill for a movement desperately needing to respond to the regime's concessions and repression campaigns.

49. F20 independent, interview by the author, Feb. 22, 2017, Rabat.
50. F20 independent, interview by the author, Jan. 19, 2017, Rabat.

The F20's Tactical Rigidity

Tactical innovation is important for movement survival. Tactical innovation refers to a diversity of protest tactics employed by social movements. Social movement studies have found that tactical innovation occurs in response to external environmental changes (like repression) or internal changes in a movement (change in actors) (Wang and Soule 2016). Social movements that change protest tactics tend to attract more attention to their cause and create new protesters (McAdam 1983). Movements that adopt multiple tactics are more likely to be successful in achieving their demands (Wang and Soule 2016, 519). Social movement scholars have also found that tactical innovation is more likely to occur when movements are united in their demands (McAdam 1983; Staggenborg 2010; Wang and Soule 2016). McAdam (2010) shows how the US civil rights movement deployed an array of tactics, including protests, freedom rides, and bus boycotts, that were effective and "very distinct in what they target and how" (Tufekci 2017, xiii). However, horizontalist movements tend to be underprepared and "unable to sustain and organize in the long term in a manner proportional to the energy they had been able to attract initially and the legitimacy they enjoyed in their demands" (Tufekci 2017, xiii).

Tactical innovation was more common during the first three months of protests (that is, protesting in different areas and holding sit-ins in front of parliament). It was, however, limited to moving protests into some popular neighborhoods and holding one protest in front of the secret Temara Detention Center (a suspected Central Intelligence Agency "black-site" torture facility), which the government repressed. Moreover, a lack of unity regarding where to demonstrate sometimes led to small protests. For instance, during a protest on May 22, 2011, some F20 activists demonstrated in front of parliament, while others protested in the popular neighborhood of Akkari where groups of protesters were dispersed by security forces.[51] Repression, therefore, was successful in dispersing protests and in convincing bystanders to avoid protests in popular neighborhoods. In

---

51. "Police Chase Moroccans Who Defied the Ban on Protests," Maghress, May 22, 2011, https://www.maghress.com/ksarsouk/4533.

other words, only parts of the F20 (typically the JCO, DWP, and radical independents) protested in popular neighborhoods. A divide between the goals among "reformist monarchists" and the "revolutionary republicans" also led to a divide regarding whether to push the movement beyond weekly protests in public areas.[52] While more revolutionary members wanted to move protests beyond public spaces to popular neighborhoods, reformists suggested that doing so would lead to unnecessary violence.[53] This disagreement led to a movement divided not only in demands but also in tactics.

An Islamist activist felt that the F20's lack of unity since March 2011 was essentially what demobilized the movement: "In my opinion, what made the F20 weak and die was disagreement in the demands. For example, we saw how it split and how some members within committee would work separately from others." The same interviewee revealed how the F20's momentum was weakening in Tangier owing to these structural issues: "Before the JCO left the F20, the movement was already weakening. There were structural reasons for this: lack of a united national organization, lack of clarity [of demands], and the lack of a plan. A movement that is confronting the state should have a plan A, B, and C. This made us lose our initiative."[54]

While independents, the USP, and the Amazigh movement adhered to the F20's initial reformist agenda and tactics, the JCO and the DWP worked together to change the F20's direction. This alliance attempted to change protest strategies by moving protests into popular neighborhoods, which were viewed as a "red line" by the state.[55] As previously discussed, mobilizing masses within popular neighborhoods was especially threatening to the regime since inhabitants from these areas tend to support

52. Reformist monarchists want to maintain the monarchy and demand reforms. Revolutionary republicans want a democratic republic without a king and have more revolutionary demands.

53. Direct and harsh repression tended to occur when the F20 experimented with entering popular neighborhoods.

54. Al-Umma and UMT member, interview by the author, Feb. 26, 2017, Tangier.

55. F20 independent, interview by the author, Oct. 26, 2017, Casablanca.

either Islamists or the king.[56] Indeed, it was at this point where the *baltagiya* (government-paid thugs and gangs) were most active (Bouhmouch 2011). The attempt by the JCO and the DWP to mobilize masses within these neighborhoods failed. Without the full support of the F20, these protests were more easily dispersed through repression. Moreover, there is little incentive for bystanders to join protests when concessions are implemented and direct repression is more widely used. Indeed, the JCO's official "Statement of Withdrawal" mentions the heavy repression that the JCO faced and laments that some F20 members (referring to reformists) limited the movement's demands and avoided pressuring the regime for "real change."[57]

Divides between the JCO-DWP coalition and the rest of the F20 fractured the movement since it could no longer form united decisions concerning where and how to protest. The participatory democracy structure of decision making through general assemblies was susceptible to organizational co-optation. Similar to multiparty coalitions that form in parliaments, general assemblies became a space for coalitions to form and control decision making of the whole movement. The JCO and the DWP were able to work together and predetermine decisions about where to protest. Since the JCO and the DWP (together) had the largest share of votes within the general assembly, they would pass decisions the two parties already agreed on outside of the assembly.[58] When other F20 activists realized that decisions were made "behind the curtains," ideological conflicts increased. In the words of a leftist activist, when decisions were

56. Islamists have been historically popular in these neighborhoods; however, with the creation of the National Initiative for Human Development in 2005, there has been more support for the king. The INDH is intended to improve living conditions in low-income areas. Interviewees along with some scholars see it as a form of clientelism, where residents get public services in exchange for supporting the king and propalace parties. See Bergh 2012.

57. "Justice and Charity Group Decides to Stop Its Participation in the February 20 Movement," Justice and Charity Group official website, https://www.aljamaa.net/ar/2011 /جماعة-العدل-والإحسان-تقرر-توقيف-مشارك/12/19/.

58. F20 independent, interview by the author, Sept. 22, 2016, Mohammedia.

predetermined by the JCO and the DWP, he realized that the F20 no longer "practiced what we preached, which means we were not democratic in the decision-making process and the planning of the protests."[59] Leftists from the USP also realized that the committees they once controlled were becoming obsolete, since the JCO and the DWP would coordinate decisions outside of the committees and general assemblies. For instance, the JCO and the DWP, against the will of USP members, decided to hold weekly protests in the Yacub-Al-Mansour neighborhood of Rabat: "My point of view was that the space [in front of parliament] was important, but they [the JCO and DWP] said no. So, this facilitated divides among the F20 by going to the popular neighborhoods. They also tried to change [tactics] from protests to sit-ins. I was against sit-ins. . . . Others within the national Support Committee said we should only [work with] groups that we consider democratic [referring to not working with JCO]." These conflicts not only fractured a previously united movement but also hindered the F20's ability to respond with united protest tactics. By June 2011, the F20 split into two separate movements in Agadir; the JCO and the DWP protested in popular neighborhoods, while the remaining parties stayed in public areas.[60] Although the F20 did not officially split in Rabat and Casablanca, some activists refused to partake in protests with the JCO, while others continued to protest with them. As mentioned by activists across all ideologies, the lack of a united strategy weakened the movement. This fact was especially apparent after the JCO left the F20.

The JCO's Withdrawal and the F20's "End"

The F20's tactical rigidity and inability to unite led to dwindling support for the movement and influenced the JCO's decision to leave the F20 on December 18, 2011. JCO members made it clear to me that by December 2011, the F20 had "exhausted its purpose."[61] In the words of JCO spokesman Fathallah Arsalane: "Going on protesting in the streets every Sunday

---

59. USFP leader, interview by the author, Nov. 24, 2016, Casablanca.
60. USFP leader, interview by the author, Dec. 13, 2016, Agadir.
61. JCO student activist, interview by the author, Oct. 20, 2016, Rabat.

with repetitive slogans is pointless and leads nowhere. The movement is a victim of its internal blockages [conflicts] therefore, we don't see any more margin of progress within it" (quoted in Benchemsi 2014, 229). Moreover, JCO members felt that they were unfairly excluded from meetings and attacked for their ideological beliefs. The JCO had little incentive to support a movement that was losing supporters and public support. A live-streamed online statement by Abdel Samad Obeid, a leader from the JCO Higher Council, is telling. A week after the JCO's withdrawal, Obeid informed viewers that "there are three options for any [social movement] organization . . . escalation, continuation, and to stop [participation in protests]." Obeid mentioned that the JCO hoped to continue protesting, but the "sufficient conditions" to "escalate and continue" protests within the F20 were missing. Obeid also commented on the tactical failure of the F20 to pressure the regime, since weekly protests did little to pressure the regime.[62] Obeid's statement reveals that the JCO indeed wanted to pressure the regime through new protest tactics, but it lacked the internal unity to do so.

The JCO's withdrawal on December 18, 2011, dealt a palpable blow to the F20. In the words of a JCO student activist, "The JCO was the spinal core of the F20 movement, and the proof was that, when the JCO left the movement, the F20 immediately died."[63] It is important to note that the JCO's decision to withdraw from the F20 shocked not only leftists but also JCO members who did not have a say in the organization's decisions made "at the top." One DWP member from the rural village of M'rirt describes the shock that he and JCO members felt when they read the announcement online:

I remember seeing the JCO announcement ceasing participation with the F20. In the room that I used to live in, I had guests that were JCO members. I was a leftist and would disagree with them, but they were also from M'rirt, and they visited me. So, when they read the statement, they

62. "The Withdrawal of 'Justice and Charity' from 'February 20' . . . Is It the End of the Movement?," Maghress, Dec. 26, 2011, https://www.maghress.com/almassae/147214.
63. JCO student leader, interview by the author, Oct. 20, 2016, Rabat.

were shocked. What I realized from this was that it was not a democratic decision by the JCO. This decision was from JCO leaders, because it was a decision no one expected. Even the youth of JCO did not expect it.[64]

Most interviewees suggested that the JCO's withdrawal was a surprise decision by the group's leaders that led to an immediate weakening of the F20. The JCO's official and vague online statement of withdrawal from the F20 was highly critical of the king's reforms and directly labeled the government as corrupt, as despotic, and as "monopolizing wealth and power"; moreover, the statement criticized the international community's support of the regime.[65]

Although the specific reasons behind the JCO withdrawal are nebulous, interviewees made it clear that ideological conflicts certainly played a big role in the decision. A report in the Moroccan newspaper *Hespress* notes that tensions between the USP and the JCO were very clear by mid-August 2011 and that the JCO realized its goals differed from many in the F20, while the USP believed that the JCO was "using the movement to overthrow the regime" (Kahl 2011). Another report claims that in October 2011, there were cases of physical harassment and fights between JCO members and independent leftists since the JCO began chanting religious slogans.[66] According to a JCO member from Casablanca, conflicts about the demands of the movement led to the "departure of the JCO and therefore the destruction and weakening of the F20."[67] Other leftists expressed a link between the PJD victory and the JCO's decision to withdraw from the movement: "The activity of the F20 became frozen after the PJD came into power, and at that point it is understood that the conflicts that the JCO fabricated froze the F20's activities in order to give the PJD an opportunity in the government."[68] Other leftists speculated about an unsubstantiated

64. Al-Naj leader from M'rirt, interview by the author, Oct. 13, 2016, Rabat.

65. Statement found at http://www.aljamaa.net/fr/document/4134.shtml. Accessed Apr. 15, 2017.

66. "Activists from February 20 Accuse JCO Members of Calling Them Infidels," *Hespress*, Oct. 24, 2011, https://www.hespress.com/politique/39934.html.

67. JCO member, interview by the author, Nov. 4, 2016, Ain Sebaa.

68. Amazigh leader, interview by the author, Oct. 4, 2016, Rabat.

"behind-the-scene deal" between the JCO and the PJD: "They [the JCO] boycotted the constitution[69] and the elections, but we are sure that some of them voted for the PJD. So, when the PJD won, they [the JCO] thought to give their friends a chance and they withdrew [from F20]."[70] It should be noted that some PJD members have had ties with the Salafists and the JCO. For instance, then minister of justice Mostafa Ramid represented Salafist prisoners in 2011 (Cretois 2017).

Interviewees across the ideological spectrum expressed that the JCO's withdrawal was the final and most direct blow to the movement and that the F20 disappeared after the JCO withdrew. Furthermore, the JCO's withdrawal was especially surprising in cities where Islamists had a considerably large presence. For instance, the largest protests occurred in Tangier, which was because of the historically large presence of Islamists in Tangier and the marginalized popular neighborhood of Beni Mekada. In other cities, where ideological cleavages were more palpable, the JCO's withdrawal was welcomed by some leftists.[71]

The JCO's withdrawal depleted the F20's power on the street, and ideological divides among "leftist" and "Islamic" camps were becoming increasingly contentious within the F20 prior to their withdrawal. Fundamental and historical distrust of Islamists by many leftists isolated the JCO. A prominent JCO leader emphasized to me that the group did indeed feel marginalized and isolated by leftists.[72] As demonstrated, many leftists felt that the JCO began to take control of the movement and were especially displeased with the JCO's increasingly gender-divided protests and religious slogans. Moreover, the F20's initial decision to delay conversations about ideology allowed the regime to easily exploit divisions within the F20. A USFP member claimed his party knew the internal ideological contradictions would not be resolved, which is partly why the USFP was one of the first parties to depart from the F20: "We concluded that the reason for not guaranteeing its sustainability was the ideological clash;

69. The JCO boycotted the constitutional referendum.
70. CDT Union MP, interview by the author, Jan. 13, 2017, Rabat.
71. USFP member, interview by the author, Dec. 13, 2016, Agadir.
72. JCO leader, interview by the author, Oct. 31, 2016, Rabat.

the different groups did not use the same compass: some wanted to head for the North and others the South. In other words, they did not have the same vision. So, there were essential differences that could not guarantee the sustainability of the movement."[73] The internal co-optation of the movement by the JCO was a product of the F20's structureless organization and vulnerability to co-optation. Internal conflicts were initially political in nature—between revolutionary elements (the JCO and DWP) and reformists (the USP, USFP, and some independents)—regarding the F20's strategy and demands. As we have seen, conflicts became increasingly ideologically based, with some leftists arguing for the removal of the JCO from the movement altogether. The JCO-DWP coalition was a political alliance that led to these highly contentious ideologically based conflicts and culminated in the withdrawal of the JCO.

Conclusion

The F20's structure facilitated internal co-optation, tactical rigidity, and the departure of the JCO. The JCO's alliance with the DWP essentially allowed both organizations to affect the F20's agenda and tactics. The JCO and the DWP attempted, unsuccessfully, to unite F20 activists and move protests into volatile popular neighborhoods. The movement was essentially unable to change its predictable tactics, while protests that did occur outside of public spaces were quickly dispersed via repression. Independent, USP, and Amazigh activists tended to stand firm with the F20's initial reformist agenda and strategy. The JCO and the DWP adopted more revolutionary demands and attempted to change protest tactics. All of these events heightened internal conflicts and culminated in the JCO's withdrawal from the F20.

A secondary finding of this chapter is that mutual interests can unite parties with competing ideological outlooks. The JCO and the DWP each have their own ideological frameworks, but they are also both illegal organizations that reject formal institutions and seek a future without a monarchy. The revolutionary demands of the JCO and the DWP put them

73. USFP leader, interview by the author, Nov. 24, 2016, Casablanca.

at odds with the reformist orientation of the F20, making their cooperation possible. Marxist-Islamist cooperation was made possible by avoiding
discussions about sensitive topics. Discussions about the place of religion
within society or women's rights were not held between JCO and DWP
members. When I asked my interviewees about the decision to table contentious issues, interviewees offered the vague response that the "people
should decide." This statement implies that interviewees agreed on democratic ideals, but also reveals an understanding between the JCO and the
DWP that their coalition was made possible by not discussing ideology.

The F20 was already declining in numbers before the JCO's withdrawal.
However, by December 2011, the F20 had little support by independent
activists.[74] This idea is demonstrated by the fact that the F20 essentially
disappeared following the JCO's withdrawal. By 2012 the JCO faced its
own crisis when Abdessalam Yassine passed away and was replaced with
his daughter, Nadia Yassine, whose image was marred by public scandals.
Some claim that the JCO's strength has steadily declined since 2011 and
has been overshadowed by the PJD (Buehler 2018, 25). Despite their current diminished status, the JCO was integral to the F20's success.

After the JCO withdrew from the F20, the movement ceased weekly
protests, and when protests did occur, they tended to be composed of radical leftists. When I asked about the size of protests following the JCO withdrawal, an F20 cofounder responded with the English idiom "peanuts."[75]
After the JCO withdrew, some independent activists attempted to give
the F20 a "new start." This time, however, independents held an anonymous "closed meeting" in late January 2012; nevertheless, the movement
never recovered from the mixed policies of the regime and the devastating
effects that they had on the F20.[76]

74. By independent support, I mean support by activists not affiliated with an organized political party.
75. F20 cofounder, interview by the author, Oct. 6, 2016, Casablanca.
76. *Hespress*, https://www.hespress.com/24-heures/44802.html.

6

The New Hirak

The Spirit of the F20 Lives

Shortly after the death of Mouchine Fikri on October 28, 2016, the F20 slogan of "Freedom, Dignity, and Social Justice" was chanted on the streets throughout the Rif region and eventually throughout the country. The Hirak-al-Rif movement, again, led to solidarity protests by Islamists, leftists, and the Amazigh cultural movement (Oumlil 2017). Prime Minister Benkirane urged members of the PJD and the Moroccan public not to protest.[1] Even Fikri's father appealed to protesters to go home and stated that Moroccans want "reform and stability" and that his son's death should not "be the cause of sedition in Morocco."[2]

Many of my planned interviews were canceled in the weeks that followed Fikri's murder; however, I was able to meet with one of Morocco's most well-known human rights activists, Reda. Reda is an outspoken critic of the regime and has faced an array of charges by the state for his activism. Reda unsuccessfully attempted to leave the country and was detained. He was eventually charged with receiving foreign money to diminish the state's image. Two days before, Reda gave an interview and asserted that he would take to the streets to protest Fikri's death.

In spite of the heightened threats against Reda, he agreed to meet me at a café in the wealthy neighborhood of Agdal in Rabat and insisted that

---

1. "Morocco Protests after Fisherman Crushed to Death in a Garbage Truck," *Guardian*, Oct. 31, 2016, https://www.theguardian.com/world/2016/oct/31/morocco-protests-after-fisherman-crushed-to-death-in-a-garbage-truck.

2. *Hespress* video, Nov. 1, 2016, https://www.hespress.com/videos/326850.html.

he not remain anonymous in the interview. Once I arrived at the café, I called Reda and was informed "another person would meet me." After waiting five minutes, a young university student and another middle-aged man who was sitting in the café briefly introduced themselves and told me to walk with them. We walked a few blocks away from the café, and they informed me that the police wanted to either arrest or speak with Reda. After a few more minutes of waiting, Reda arrived and introduced himself and said jokingly that "you are *really* doing fieldwork now"—an apparent reference to the unexpected situation I found myself in. Eventually, we walked another three blocks together to the same café. Reda mentioned that it was not the best time for an interview, but insisted I stay.

When we arrived at the café, Reda told me that he was waiting for two journalists to arrive. I thought that it was maybe to report his arrest. Reda lamented that he was, again, not allowed to leave the country and, again, on trial for various charges. I was told by the law student that these recent charges stemmed from a protest that Reda partook in two days before. I offered, repeatedly, to reschedule our meeting, but Reda insisted that I stay and ask what I could. About twenty minutes into the interview, I could tell that Reda was expecting to be arrested. He gave around two hundred euros to his older friend, along with his credit cards. At that moment, a police officer entered the café, and Reda said, "Here they are," and pulled out his ID—apparently assuming the officer was going to arrest him. The police officer walked past us and went upstairs to another section of the café. Reda indicated that this encounter may have been a coincidence, since "they always come in pairs when they arrest someone." Later, the police officer left the café, and the young university student and his friend kept an eye on him when he left. The fear was palpable at that moment.

When the journalists came, I was told to turn off my recorder. Reda left with the journalists, and I was left alone in the café with the young university student. The young man expressed the obvious: "everything has changed" since the protests that occurred two days earlier. I did, indeed, quickly realize that after the Hirak protests, some interviewees were harder to get in touch with and that the fear of arrest, repression, or public smearing by the state was, again, an imminent reality for many well-known F20 activists.

Hirak-al-Rif: Revolt from Periphery to Nation

The F20 changed Moroccan activism. However, the roots of the Hirak-al-Rif date back to the marginalization of the Rif region since independence and arguably since the anticolonial struggle for a Riffian state.[3] Indeed, shortly after Moroccan independence, King Hassan II (then crown prince) crushed the 1958 Riffian Revolt. Thousands were killed through indiscriminate bombings of villages, while women were raped by the Forces Armées Royales (Maddy-Weitzman 2011, 86). Rebellions have continued in the Rif since 1958. Notably, in 1984 students and the unemployed rioted throughout Morocco, but especially in the Rif.[4] King Hassan reminded the Rif of the state's reaction to Riffian dissent by threatening that "the people of the North have previously known the violence of the crown prince; it will be best for them not to know that of the king's" (Mouline 2015, 1). Repression and regional neglect were the centerpiece to King Hassan II's stance toward the Rif. King Hassan II avoided visiting the Rif and downplayed past atrocities by the state (Maddy Weitzman 2011, 86).

King Mohammed VI assumed the thrown in 1999 and took a different approach to the Rif. Unlike his father, King Mohammed frequently visited the Rif and, after a 2004 earthquake ravaged the region, invested money into infrastructure projects (Maddy-Weitzman 2011, 156). Moreover, Maddy-Weitzman notes that the Truth and Reconciliation Commission formed by the king did not have an explicit "Berber agenda," but indeed most victims were Amazigh (2011, 155). Even prior to Tamazight being made an official state language in 2011, Amazigh history and the Tamazight language were introduced in school textbooks. Despite the increased attention paid to the Rif, the region remains neglected, and unemployment is high among youth compared to other parts of the country (Masbah 2017).

As may be clear, the Riffian region is rooted in historical marginalization and neglect and is distinct from the central goals of the F20.

3. The short-lived Riffian Republic was established in 1921, but Spain and France successfully took the territory in 1926.

4. "Discontent behind the Image of Calm in Morocco," Socialist Worker, Jan. 25, 2017, https://socialistworker.org/2017/01/25/discontent-behind-the-image-of-calm.

Nevertheless, many activists do believe that the F20 paved the way for the Hirak-al-Rif by demonstrating that the Rif's marginalization is not solely a regional issue but a national one. Some attribute this opinion to a growing distrust in state institutions and a recognition that state institutions beyond the palace are powerless (Diouani 2021). Others note that the Hirak-al-Rif resonated with all Moroccans through the concept of *al-hogra*—an Arabic term that broadly highlights contempt, degradation, and injustice (Ilahiane 2019). This contention is evidenced by the fact that protests against *al-hogra* continued throughout Morocco until 2018.

Unlike previous waves of dissent in the Rif, the 2016 Hirak-al-Rif uprising tended to resonate with activists throughout the country, with sit-ins and demonstrations in solidarity with the Rif occurring throughout Morocco (Rachidi 2017). In essence, it is clear that the Hirak-al-Rif is historically a regional struggle; however, activists highlight an important link between the F20 and the ongoing Hirak-al-Rif. As we will see, activists namely highlight a new "culture of street politics" along with a recognition by Hirak-al-Rif activists that their movement should move away from the decentralized social movement structure adopted by the F20.

The Spirit of F20 Lives: The New Culture of Street Politics

> The F20 left its spirit in Morocco. People now protest over water, electricity, and living conditions.
> —DWP activist in Rabat

> Corruption and the power dynamics of the regime persist, but the spirit of the F20 continues.
> —JCO member in Ain Sebaa

Most interviews I conducted concluded the same way: with the interviewee expressing that the F20 did not figuratively die and that its spirit lives on. Interviewees often expressed how the F20 changed Moroccan politics by initiating a new "culture of street protests," as now evidenced by the Hirak movement in the northern Rif region of Morocco. In the words of one interviewee who is highly pessimistic of any reforms put forth by the regime: "The F20 movement did not change Morocco. It changed Moroccans." The culture of protests that followed the 2011 MENA Uprisings in

Morocco is defended as the biggest accomplishment of the F20. This culture includes small-scale microrebellions (that is, standing up to police) and large-scale movements (such as the Hirak movement). The same leader of the AMDH quoted above was optimistic about how individual citizens changed following the F20: "The simple citizen is no longer scared of administrators, guards, and police; they now can stand up and face the system. The movement does not remain in the form of protests, but it created ideas and changed ways of thinking and expressing anger."[5] Similarly, a JCO student leader expressed optimism that there is no longer fear to confront authorities and point out injustices: "Moroccans used to fear police brutality if they protest, but now the F20 movement has given the Moroccan people the strength to protest and demonstrate. We can say that breaking the wall of fear is the biggest victory in the history of Morocco. That people nowadays can say *no* and express their opinions and thoughts."[6] Another JCO member agreed that this freedom of expression was the biggest accomplishment of the movement: "Within the JCO, we think that the biggest accomplishment the F20 had was that it broke the barrier of fear among Moroccans. . . . [T]he F20 did not die; it may have changed, but its spirit continues."[7] Others even expressed the sentiment that the relationship between authorities and the people improved owing to the F20. For instance, an F20 independent activist felt that the F20 and the advent of social media helped create an environment where the regime listens and acts on grievances by the people:

> I think the spirit of the F20 movement is still here. The point is not to go out and have thousands of people in the street. People now are monitoring public politics through the internet and Facebook and Twitter and the press. Even the authorities are smarter today. They follow what happens on social media. They try to solve everything that can create problems before people go out on the streets. Like what happened

5. Ex-leader of AMDH, interview by the author, Oct. 5, 2016, Rabat.
6. JCO student leader, interview by the author, Oct. 20, 2016, Rabat.
7. JCO member, interview by the author, Dec. 28, 2016, Casablanca.

in Al-Hoceima with the fishmonger's death: Morocco can explode at any moment, but the police try to pay attention to these things before they occur. This is nice. This happens in America, too. It's nice that the authorities care about what the youth write on social media. This is a good thing.[8]

During my fieldwork, I quickly learned that using the term *death* in describing what happened to the F20 often led to emotional responses about how the movement never "died" but rather changed into other movements with different names and goals. I learned to use the subtler term of *decline* regarding the movement. Indeed, many activists considered the Hirak movement to be a continuation of the F20; however, key differences between the movements are clear.

The horizontally organized F20 movement was not a unified movement. The political and ideological tensions among activists were clear, with especially defined divisions between reformists and revolutionaries. Unlike the F20, the Hirak movement united the northern Rif region through a shared Riffian-Amazigh identity. The demonstrators in the Hirak did not raise Moroccan flags during protests, but rather flew Amazigh and Rif Republic flags, along with pictures of Abdelkarim al-Khattabi—the rebel founder of the short-lived Rif Republic. Masbah also notes that the Hirak activists "established achievable social and political demands early on. From the outset, the movement's activists drafted a list of demands, including the right to a fair trial, demilitarization of the Rif, encouraging investment and infrastructure development, as well as the construction of a university, hospital, and a cancer treatment center in the region" (2017, 4). Moreover, the Hirak learned from the F20's "tactical standstill." Rather, the Hirak employed a "wide range of tactics and forms of protest" that "helps explain Hirak al-Rif's success in organizing over 700 events, including demonstrations, vigils, and protests" (Masbah 2017, 5). Another innovative "repertoire of contention" adopted by the Hirak was the *chenten*, which is essentially a flash-mob protest that is live-streamed on social

8. Former TV journalist and independent F20 activist, interview by the author, Jan. 13, 2017, Rabat.

media within densely populated residential areas and known to grow in numbers very quickly (Jebnoun 2020). Hirak activists effectively attracted the international coverage of their cause that the F20 lacked. For instance, protests occurred in Marrakech at the widely anticipated COP 22 Conference—the United Nations' annual climate-change conference. One activist held a banner that read: "Welcome to COP22, We Grind People Here" (Beaumont 2016). These demonstrations in Marrakech tarnished the image of the regime, and in the words of one activist, Moroccans felt that the "state is using this conference to greenwash its abuses, to greenwash the economic, social and environmental injustices that the people of Morocco face." The palace, again, used familiar strategies to ward off protests in Marrakech, including smear campaigns on social media that accused activists of "being un-Islamic and trying to turn Morocco into Syria" (Shearlaw 2016).

The Hirak also began moving away from the F20's decentralized and horizontal structure and toward a more organized movement led by the charismatic Al-Hoceima native Nasser Zifzafi. Zifzafi, who was previously an F20 activist, not only was able to unite the Rif behind his speeches demanding greater state investment in the northern region, but also railed against an issue affecting many other Moroccans: *al-hogra*. The North African term broadly refers to lack of dignity faced by many in the region. The Hirak, like the F20, lacked a united decision-making body, but it did have Zifzafi as its leader, and he tended to direct the movement's slogans and demands. Zifzafi has appealed to Moroccans beyond the Rif by refuting separatism and repeatedly called on all Moroccans to demonstrate against the regime (Paolini 2017). According to Monjib, Zifzafi effectively united competing political forces, since "he is neither explicitly Islamic nor secular, nor exclusively leftist or rightist. . . . What makes for the cohesion of Zifzafi's discourse and the unity of the movement he leads is not ideological, but political: the dignity of the population through the recognition its socio-economic rights, the end of the 'oppressive Makhzen' and its moral defeat" (2020, 127). Wolf also notes that "the Hirak movement in the Rif has demonstrated a much higher degree of persistence and unity" (2019, 1).

The state, this time, reacted to the Hirak with more repressive measures. This reaction is partly owing to the clear leadership structures of the movement, but also because of the directly confrontational discourse by activists. Zifzafi and other Riffian leaders were not just victims of online smear campaigns (accused of being spies or being funded by foreign entities), but also directly charged with crimes that essentially left the leaders of Hirak imprisoned. Zifzafi was arrested on May 29, 2017, and was ultimately given a twenty-year sentence for an array of charges, including threatening state security and disrespecting the king. By June 2017, more than four hundred activists were imprisoned, some given sentences of twenty years. Journalists were also targeted. Eight journalists covering the Hirak were arrested and imprisoned on various charges, including "inviting people to participate in a banned demonstration" (Reporters without Borders 2017). Perhaps the most infamous case is that of independent journalist and founder of Badil.info Hamid El Mahdaoui, who was arrested for alleged involvement in the Hirak and served four years in prison. El Mahdaoui was dubiously charged with "failing to report a security threat" (Human Rights Watch 2018). Most recently, F20 cofounder and Hirak activist Omar Radi had his phone and computer targeted by sophisticated spyware and is now facing an array of charges, including "undermining state security" (Amnesty International 2020).

Some conclude the state's more repressive stance toward the Hirak may be owing to the region's marginalization and the subsequent distrust of the central state (Wolf 2019). The state also recognized the threat posed by Zifzafi's leadership, which is why he was sentenced to twenty years in prison—including one year in solitary confinement. Zifzafi's revolutionary tone and unwavering demands were a clear shift from the initially reformist demands of the F20. Indeed, Zifzafi "was one of the rare exceptions" in Morocco, since "he spoke freely" (Monjib 2020, 125). Perhaps the most well-known example of this freedom of speech is when Zifzafi confronted an imam in Al-Hoceima for serving the regime instead of God. In a country where the king is the "commander of the faithful," this encounter had riveting implications, including directly challenging the king's religious legitimacy (Jebnoun 2019).

Jebnoun notes that the F20 was an "urban movement unable to bridge the urban-rural divide or engage with local dynamics in the rural areas where the imperatives of economic development, social justice,

and regional inequalities have been prioritized over political demands"
(2019, 51). Indeed, many Amazigh activists I interviewed did not feel
their movement's interests were adequately represented in the F20 movement, which tended to focus major protests in large cities. One Amazigh
activist from the Rif, lamented, "In general, the demands in Rabat would
spread to other F20 committees in other cities."[9] An Islamist activist from
Tangier believed that the geographic proximity to Europe, and contentious history with the Moroccan state, both explain why Tangier and
other northern Moroccan cities have been so restive during F20 protests:
"Youth in the Rif are exposed to Spanish TV and radio and often com-
pare their situation with that in nearby Spain. . . . [T]hey think, 'They
have made it, but we have not.'" He explained Moroccans in the North see
that Spain's transition from an underdeveloped dictatorial monarchy to a
developed democracy "brings more people out to the streets."[10] The interviewee pointed out that you can see Spain from the Strait of Gibraltar,
and many youths in Tangier see their future in Spain and not in Morocco.
Another Amazigh activist from Tetouan believed the "Amazigh movement paid a price" within the F20, since nationalization of private lands
in the Rif increased after 2011.[11] The same Amazigh leader believed that
the F20 activists from Rabat were not concerned with regional issues in
the Rif: "The leftists in the F20 from Rabat do not know what is happening
in Tangier or Al-Hoceima, but not the Amazigh movement, because the
Amazigh movement is federalist in nature."

Most activists from the Amazigh movement made it clear that they
were never comfortable participating with Islamist organizations, especially the JCO. One Amazigh leader based in Rabat echoed a common sentiment among Amazigh activists regarding Islamists: "We always see the
Amazigh movement as opposing the demands of the Islamists, because
we don't consider that there are moderate or extreme Islamists. If you
have ideas built in religion, then you spoil the ideas of democracy. . . . The

---

9. Amazigh activist, interview by the author, Oct. 5, 2016, Rabat.

10. UMT and Hizb al-Umma member, interview by the author, Feb. 26, 2016, Tangier.

11. Amazigh leader, interview by the author, Dec. 8, 2016, Rabat.

Amazigh movement within the F20 feared the Islamist presence in the movement. . . . The Amazigh movement is always in opposition to the Islamist movements because the Amazigh movement believes that we cannot talk about a democratic state without a true separation between religion and state."[12] It is important to note that the "Amazigh movement" is not united in its stance toward religion. Indeed, Nasser Zifzafi and other Riffian activists adopted religious overtones to their slogans and demands. For example, Zifzafi criticized Rabat's annual Mawazine Music Festival as anti-Islamic.[13] It is not surprising that Islamists, like the JCO, have again mobilized national marches in support of the Hirak (Monjib 2020).

In essence, Amazigh activists within the F20 believed they accomplished very limited goals within the movement, but it is clear that the "culture of street protests" started by the F20 helped the Hirak movement. Moreover, some of the F20's demands and slogans were again chanted by Hirak activists in 2016–17. An F20 activist from the small town of Berkane indicated that many of the Hirak's demands, like building hospitals and universities as well as investing in infrastructure, were "local demands" during F20 demonstrations in 2011.[14] Hirak activists also learned from the lessons of the F20 by being more organized and having clear and united demands. Nevertheless, the state has again outmaneuvered the Hirak by offering limited concessions followed by massive and more widespread repression of activists. The king was again "forced" to intervene and demanded an investigation into Fikri's death, which led to the arrest and sentencing of eleven individuals. Most recently, the king issued a royal decree to pardon dozens of Hirak activists; Zifzafi, however, remains in prison and conducted a hunger strike in August 2020. This concession was facilitated by the fact that the movement now has leaders to target via smear campaigns and harsh prison sentences. Finally, it is important to note that the unprecedented reforms by the state in 2011 are still fresh in

12. Amazigh leader, interview by the author, Sept. 30, 2016, Rabat.

13. "Police in Morocco Hunt Protest Leader in Rif Region," *National News*, May 26, 2017, https://www.thenationalnews.com/world/police-in-morocco-hunt-protest-leader-in-rif-region-1.77045.

14. Talea member from Berkane, interview by the author, Dec. 2, 2016, Rabat.

the minds of the public, which may explain why the Hirak tended to be more successful in amassing protests in the Rif.

Conclusion

Demonstrations after 2016 occurred throughout Morocco, and both Hirak-al-Rif activists and F20 activists have faced harsher repression. At the time of writing, some of the most well-known F20 activists are jailed without due process, including Reda, who was charged with, among other things, "threatening state security." Other prominent activists are arrested under unrelated issues, including supposed abortion (Abouzzohour 2020). Most recently, at least thirty activists were sentenced with jail terms for violating the "State of Medical Emergency," which placed restrictions on movement to curb the spread of COVID-19 (Karam 2020). The Brookings Institution has noted the "sharp turn towards repression" since 2016 and highlights the belief the regime may be turning toward repression owing to the worsening socioeconomic situation since 2011, which has spurred increased popular unrest (Karam 2020). Others have noted that the turn toward increased repression may be because of increasing willingness to criticize not only the government but also the palace (Rachidi 2019). Indeed, what was most surprising in Zifzafi's speeches was that they were directed at the king (Diouani 2021). This factor may highlight the reality that once "red lines" are crossed, repression is the only viable response. This reality has very important implications for the findings in this book, especially considering that the king's reformist image may be deteriorating.

As outlined throughout the book, policy precedent matters. The Moroccan king's strategy of concessions followed by limited repression quelled protests in Morocco and rests on the historical reality that the "reformist king" goes through with announced concessions and does not rely exclusively on repression to quell dissent. This dynamic explains why reforms announced by Hosni Mubarak, Ali Abdullah Saleh, or Bashar al-Assad did not effectively quell dissent. Whether the reformist trend of the Moroccan king will be maintained in the future remains unclear; however, increased repression since 2016 suggests that the king's concessionary approach to dissent is changing.

Conclusion

A dynamic and interconnected series of events facilitated the decrease of protests in Morocco. The increased repression against the F20 in May 2011; the passing of the constitutional referendum in July 2011; the early general elections on November 25, 2011; and the election results announced two weeks later all facilitated protest abatement. These events signaled that change was being implemented and that certain "red lines" should not be crossed. These events created new discussions within the F20 and among the public concerning the future of the movement.

This book demonstrates that the Moroccan regime's use of a mixed policy—offering concessions followed by repression—lessened protests. It further shows that such a strategy is successful because of three main conditions. First, the Moroccan regime has a history of declaring and implementing reforms. Second, a sequence of concessions signaled that the F20's grievances were being addressed. Third, the regime's repression against the F20 led to a perceived disunity between the goals of the movement and the general public. The mixed policy used by the regime during the 2011 MENA Uprisings caused the F20 to demobilize through a lack of public support and by highlighting internal ideological cleavages. This decline resulted in the movement's demobilization and alienation from society. With the movement internally fractured and perceived as more revolutionary and radical in tone, the public was no longer convinced of the need for a social movement, especially since a series of unprecedented reforms were already being implemented.

The main goal of this book has been to understand how these mixed policies affect the internal dynamics of a social movement, resulting in the

movement's demobilization. King Mohammed VI's consistent accommodative policies led to the F20's demobilization; however, concessions were
also followed by repression, which is becoming more common since the
Hirak movement started. The mixing of concessions with repression, and
its consequences, is understudied. The March 9 speech initiated a framing conflict between "reformist monarchists" and more "revolutionary
republicans" within the F20. As the F20's tone became more revolutionary, the regime strategically smeared the F20 as radical and disconnected
from average Moroccans. The Moroccan state consistently conveyed those
unprecedented concessions would be implemented, while the F20 was
perceived as extremist and internally co-opted as well as unnecessary
since reforms were being implemented. Accommodative and repressive
policies worked in this case because the regime signaled to the public that
grievances were being met. These signals included addressing grievances
in March 2011, implementing proposed reforms in June 2011, creating a
referendum vote where more than 70 percent of the populace voted yes
in July 2011, and finally allowing sidelined and popular Islamists to win a
parliamentary plurality by not meddling in elections in August 2011. The
victory of the PJD had an especially palpable effect on the movement. Even
hard-line opponents of the PJD admitted that its victory ceased the F20's
protest momentum.

Following each of these concessions, the F20 became increasingly dele-
gitimized by the public, and internal fracturing persisted. The movement
was tactically stationary since effective decision-making structures were
missing and since political organizations, like the JCO, became increasingly influential. The JCO partnership with the DWP led to increased
ideological conflicts—with some leftists calling for the removal of the
JCO from the F20. This Islamist-Marxist alliance also allowed the JCO
to dominate F20 committees and general assemblies. This finding demonstrates that influential political organizations can co-opt and control
horizontalist movements. The F20 was initially a movement controlled by
independent activists, but influential political organizations eventually
dominated the movement. Essentially, the F20 could never overcome its
internal fracturing, a fracturing that became especially visible after the
March 9 speech and the 2011 general elections.

Lessons

The Moroccan case is unique since concessions were the initial response of the regime, while most other regimes in 2011 responded with a mix of repressive measures followed by empty promises of reform. In Tunisia, Egypt, and Libya, repression was used within a week of protest inception in 2011. However, the case of Jordan shares a lot of similarities with Morocco. Both countries have popular long-serving monarchs, and both responded to mass demonstrations in 2011 with concessions followed by limited repression. Scholars have claimed that strong historical-religious claims to legitimacy allow a monarchy to remain stable during protests (Bank, Richter, and Sunik 2015). Although there is merit to this argument, which is most clearly evidenced by the fact that most demands by protest movements were reformist (reforming the constitution) and not revolutionary (regime overthrow), the case of the F20 demonstrates how the line between reformist and revolutionary can be crossed. Indeed, slogans such as "The monarchy is rotten—listen, Mohamed VI, soon it's your turn," and even "The people want the downfall of the regime" were chanted during the F20 protests (Hoffman and König 2013, 1). King Hussein of Jordan (King Abdullah II's father), like other Arab executives, has survived military coup attempts (Yom and Gause 2012). Most recently, King Abdullah's half brother Prince Hamzah bin Hussein led a failed coup attempt against the monarch—alleging that the country's leaders were corrupt and incompetent.[1]

In essence, historical-religious legitimacy alone cannot ensure that future movements in monarchies are strictly reformist in nature. The Moroccan king's decision to offer and implement reforms, to use calculated and limited repression, and to allow the PJD to win elections were all necessary factors that helped maintain the stability of the monarch. His monarchical legitimacy alone was not sufficient to prevent mass contention and, in some cases, calls for his ouster. The same case can be made for Jordan; however, important differences exist.

1. "Jordan's Prince Hamzah bin Hussein 'under House Arrest," BBC, Apr. 4, 2021, https://www.bbc.com/news/world-middle-east-56626370.

In Jordan, major pre-2011 reforms occurred from 1989 to 1993 under the reign of King Hussein. These developments included parliamentary elections, lifting martial law, and legalization of political parties. Unlike the case of Morocco, major reforms ceased after this period. Moreover, rather than receiving national praise, reforms in Jordan instigated the "Jordanian Intifada," which saw riots and protests against austerity International Monetary Fund measures. King Hussein sacked the prime minister and promised reforms, but the liberalization continued. Ryan concisely outlines the state of reforms within Jordan since 1989: "Political reform, in contrast, has often faltered, stalled, stagnated, and at times regressed. There is a pattern, in short, of rising and falling reform efforts that suggests continuity even amid apparent change. Over the past several decades, for example, Jordan has experienced both liberalization and deliberalization in its political life, as the state has at times retreated from earlier reforms" (2018, 147). Like in Morocco, by 2011 activists overwhelmingly demanded constitutional reforms, but the important distinction between the two cases is that Jordan lacked the historical precedent of announcing and implementing major reforms. As Ryan outlines in his book, activists needed to "push the regime back toward the reform process" (2018, 156). This phenomenon was not the case in Morocco. Another important distinction is that Jordan has been entrenched in regional unrest since its creation, and the threat of direct spillover of conflicts from Syria, Iraq, and the West Bank has forced opposition to tone down activism and "tread warily and with unease" (Ryan 2018, 22). This unsettling reality may explain why protests in Jordan during 2011–12 tended to be small and sporadic and to self-disperse after a few hours. Despite the important differences, the Moroccan case does inform the Jordanian case by highlighting that public perception about the legitimacy of reforms is important. Said differently, Morocco's mixed policy rested on overwhelming faith in the monarchy's reformist king announcing and implementing major reforms.

Most recently, Algeria's "Revolution of Smiles" highlights the social learning among regimes since 2011. President Abdelaziz Bouteflika, who had been in power for nearly twenty years, was forced to step down six days after massive protests started on February 16, 2019. In 2011 Bouteflika used the state's oil resources to crush dissent, while also promising reforms (Chikhi 2011). Subsequent elections have been marred by corruption scandals, and repeated constitutional amendments extended the ailing president's term limits. By 2019 his promise to stand down was met with ongoing demonstrations.[2] The military, recognizing that Bouteflika's concessions would not quell dissent, quickly moved to remove the leader from power (Nossiter 2019). Again, we see mass protests forcing a long-standing autocrat to step down; however, what is interesting in this case is that the regime did not resort to the familiar policy of mass repression, and, in contrast to the events of 2011, the revolution was relatively peaceful. Nevertheless, the Algerian Hirak movement continues to hold demonstrations for democratic reforms, and most Algerians boycotted the country's first parliamentary elections since ousting Bouteflika on April 2, 2019. At the time of writing, it is unclear how the Algerian Hirak movement will demobilize, but I foresee regimes will learn the lessons from the 2011 MENA Uprisings and increasingly rely on a mixed policy of concessions and repression to quell dissent. Social movement structure and a regime's past policies toward political opposition will be important when judging why they are successful or not.

Limitations

Despite the findings in the book, limitations need to be addressed. It is important to note that I was fortunate to gain access to closed activist networks throughout Morocco. However, my sample did not include the voices of all women. I quickly found that women interviewees within Islamist networks, especially the JCO, are especially difficult to access. On two occasions male JCO interviewees made it clear that interviewing women from the organization would be difficult unless I got permission from their husbands and only if they were present during the interview. I was unsuccessful at interviewing any women from these organizations. Given the importance of the JCO within the F20, and Moroccan politics

---

2. "Algeria: President Bouteflika Finally Promises to Stand Down," *DW News*, Nov. 3, 2019, https://www.dw.com/en/algeria-president-bouteflika-finally-promises-to-stand-down/a-47860906.

generally, interviewing women from this organization would have led to a more representative sample. Research informed by this hidden population will further help distill social movement demobilization within ideologically diverse movements.

Another important limitation of the book is the lack of public polls concerning perceptions of the F20 specifically. Given that the argument of the book partly rests on alignment between public opinion and a social movement, it is important to understand what the public thought about the F20 from 2011 to 2012. In the book, interviews and secondary sources highlight the disparity between public opinion and the direction that the F20 was taking. Unfortunately, public opinion polls specifically concerning the F20 from 2011 to 2012 are unavailable. Nevertheless, Arab Barometer and the Arab Center for Research and Policy Studies polls were cited, especially to show the faith Moroccans had in constitutional reforms. Going forward, more research is needed to more accurately measure perceptions about the need of social movements, not by activists but by the public. Given that social movements occur over the realm of the public, future research should use surveys to measure public perceptions about social movements.

Future of Social Movement Studies

Since the 1980s, there has been a shift in the study of contentious politics away from the classical social psychological approach, which tends to focus more on how frustration and aggression lead to mobilization (Gurr 2015; Gurney and Tierney 1982).[3] Instead, structural perspectives, like resource mobilization and political process theories, focus more on the environmental drivers that facilitate or suppress social movements (Aminzade and McAdam 2001, 14). In other words, advantageous or disadvantageous political environments (openness or closure of political system, presence of elite allies, or a state's capacity for repression) along with organizational strength are better predictors of successful social movements (McAdam

---

3. Relative deprivation theory, for example, argues that protests can occur when people are deprived of something they feel entitled to.

1983; Tarrow 1994; Meyer and Minkoff 2004). Scholars from this tradition tended to focus on the rise of movements as the result of variations in structural opportunities (Tarrow and Tilly 2003).

In the 1990s, scholars began to incorporate culture into their theories; however, these scholars tended to limit culture to the effects of framing techniques on social movements (Snow and Benford 1988, 1992). The literature has only recently recognized that internal movement dynamics are important: "We have come to think of interpersonal networks, interpersonal communication, and various forms of continuous negotiation—including the negotiation of identities—as figuring centrally in the dynamics of contention" (Tarrow and Tilly 2009, 9). Social movement theorists (across all approaches) have long analyzed why movements occur, but less attention has been paid to deterrence and de-escalation, or what some term the *demobilization* of social movements (Davenport 2015). McAdam, McCarthy, and Zald claim that social movement theorists have "underdeveloped knowledge about the dynamics of collective action past the emergence of a movement" and that this lack is a "glaring deficiency in the literature" (1988, 728).

This book has combined structural and cultural approaches by looking at how changes in structure (concessions and repression) affect internal movement framing, discussions, and tactics. In other words, the structural is tied to internal movement dynamics, and by considering both, we can better understand why movements mobilize and demobilize. Moreover, this project has focused exclusively on this underresearched line of study that focuses on movement decline and demobilization. To be clear, there is an area of study that specifically analyzes demobilization. However, studies specific to the demobilization of social movements are usually limited to cases where only repression is studied. This book demonstrates that concessions can trigger mechanisms that lead to movement demobilization. Using concessions as a first response to mass protests has implications for how effective repression is as well.

More research concerning the relationship between concessions, repression, and protest demobilization is needed. How the structure of movements interacts with these factors matters too. The recent trend of less structured, horizontally organized, and leaderless movements is by no means limited to the MENA region. Rather, similar movements are occurring throughout the world, and this point is important because the relationship between state policies and social movements is changing (Tufekci 2017). How state policies demobilize movements without clear leadership structure merits more study. In Morocco, for example, the regime's decision to repress the JCO during March 2011 led to increased internal conflicts about the "invisibility" of Islamists within the F20. Following the JCO's targeting by the regime in March 2011, the JCO became more visible within the media, chanted religious slogans, and raised religious banners—a break from the F20's initial agreement. Tufekci (2017) argues that because horizontalist movements lack structure, they will likely falter and die down quickly, but she does not explain why some movements demobilize after initial goals are achieved (that is, the overthrow of presidents in Tunisia and Egypt) and others are successfully defeated through concessions or repression before they realize all of their goals (the case of the F20). Essentially, more studies need to focus on why and how social movements demobilize.

The theoretical contribution of this project assists future studies of demobilization by helping demonstrate how accommodative and repressive policies can abate protests and demobilize movements. My theory demonstrates how reformist leaders, which respond to social unrest by initially addressing demands, can convince the public that demands are sufficiently met and that there is no longer a need for a social movement. Internally, social movements are affected by such policies as well. My theoretical framework demonstrates how social movements attempted to overcome the perception of "problem depletion" by changing frames, which eventually led to internal cleavages and disputes. Future scholars need to incorporate a similar logic that considers how similar policies have an important effect both among the public (which a social movement needs for support) and internally among different members of a social movement. After a public perception that initial demands are being met, then repression aimed at smearing the movement can also demobilize a movement. Smear campaigns, for example, can lead to a disunity between a social movement and the public's goals. The revolutionary tone that many F20 activists took after the concessions were offered and implemented was not widely accepted within Morocco, where the monarchy is usually seen as legitimate.

Needless to say, mixed policies of concessions and repression can have various outcomes. Contrary to Mark Lichbach's (1987) seminal finding, there need not be a consistency of adhering to one policy (concessions or repression) for protest decline and demobilization to occur. Indeed, as movements become increasingly horizontalist in nature, diverse, often ideologically contentious, groups must find ways to work together within leaderless structures. Movements without traditional leaders and collective decision-making bodies will likely need to find alternate ways to respond to a state's calculated mixed-policy approach. Going forward, I foresee this means of "social control" through mixed policy becoming more prevalent, and this book offers a theory regarding when concessions and repression can demobilize a social movement.

References

Index

References

Abdel-Samad, Mounah. 2014. "Why Reform Not Revolution: A Political Opportunity Analysis of Morocco 2011 Protests Movement." *Journal of North African Studies* 19, no. 5: 792–809.

Abend, Lisa. 2011. "Reforming Morocco: Taking Apart the King's Speech." *Time World*, Mar. 10, 2011. content.time.com/time/world/article/0,8599,2058141,00.html.

Abouzzohour, Yasmina. 2020. "Morocco's Sharp Turn towards Repression." Brookings Institution, Jan. 8, 2020. https://www.brookings.edu/opinions/moroccos-sharp-turn-toward-repression/.

Abu-Lughod, Lila. 1991. "Writing against Culture." In *Recapturing Anthropology: Working in the Present*, edited by Richard Fox, 137–62. Santa Fe, NM: School of American Research Press.

Ahrne, Göran, and Nils Brunsson. 2011. "Organization Outside Organizations: The Significance of Partial Organization." *Organization* 18, no. 1: 83–104.

Albrecht, Holger. 2005. "How Can Opposition Support Authoritarianism? Lessons from Egypt." *Democratization* 12, no. 3: 378–97.

Albrecht, Holger, and Eva Wegner. 2006. "Autocrats and Islamists: Contenders and Containment in Egypt and Morocco." *Journal of North African Studies* 11, no. 2: 123–41.

Al-Hatem, Fadwa. 2011. "Syrians Are Tired of Assad's 'Reforms.'" *Guardian*, May 31, 2011. https://www.theguardian.com/commentisfree/2011/may/31/syrians-assad-bill-fair-elections.

Alianak, Sonia L. 2014. *Transition towards Revolution and Reform: The Arab Spring Realised?* Edinburgh: Edinburgh Univ. Press.

Al-Jazeera. 2011. "المغرب يفرج عن 96 معتقلا سياسيا." Accessed Sept. 4, 2019. http://www.aljazeera.net/home/Getpage/f6451603-4dff-4ca1-9c10-122741d17432/1b3cfd4e-dd44-4f27-8132-1b7a1813f79e.

Al-Jazeera English. 2011. "Middle East Rulers Make Concessions." http://www
.aljazeera.com/news/middleeast/2011/02/201121210345525985.html.

Allilou, Aziz. 2014. "Moroccans and the 20 February Movement." *Morocco World
News*, Feb. 22, 2014. http://www.moroccoworldnews.com/2014/02/123361
/moroccans-and-the-20-february-movement/.

Alrababa'h, Ala, and Lisa Blaydes. 2021. "Authoritarian Media and Diversionary
Threats: Lessons from 30 Years of Syrian State Discourse." *Political Science
Research and Methods* 9, no. 4: 693–708.

Amar, Paul, and Vijay Prashad, eds. 2013. *Dispatches from the Arab Spring: Understanding the New Middle East*. Minneapolis: Univ. of Minnesota Press.

Aminzade, Ronald R., Jack A. Goldstone, Doug McAdam, Elizabeth J. Perry, Sidney Tarrow, William H. Sewell, and Charles Tilley. 2001. *Silence and Voice in
the Study of Contentious Politics*. Cambridge: Cambridge Univ. Press.

Aminzade, Ron, and Doug McAdam. 2001. "Emotions and Contentious Politics." In *Silence and Voice in the Study of Contentious Politics*, 14–50. Cambridge: Cambridge Univ. Press.

Amnesty International. 2020. "Omar Radi: The Moroccan Journalist Who
Won't Be Silenced." June 22, 2020. https://www.amnesty.org/en/latest/news
/2020/06/omar-radi-moroccan-journalist-refuses-to-be-silenced/.

Amnesty International USA. 2011. "Amnesty International Urges Morocco Not
to Suppress Weekend Protests." Mar. 27, 2011. https://www.amnestyusa
.org/press-releases/amnesty-international-urges-morocco-not-to-suppress
-weekend-protests-2/.

Andreopoulos, G., and Z. F. K. Arat. 2014. "On the Uses and Misuses of Human
Rights: A Critical Approach to Advocacy." In *The Uses and Misuses of Human
Rights*, 1–27. New York: Palgrave Macmillan.

Arab Barometer. 2013. Arab Barometer II. https://www.arabbarometer.org/survey
-data/.

———. 2017. "Morocco Five Years after the Arab Uprisings: Findings from the
Arab Barometer." https://www.arabbarometer.org/.

Arieff, Alexis. 2013. "Morocco: Current Issues." *Congressional Research Service*
(Oct.): 1–17.

———. 2017. "Morocco: Current Issues." *Current Politics and Economics of Africa* 10, no. 3: 317–41.

Badran, Sammy Zeyad. 2014. "The Contentious Roots of the Egyptian Revolution." *Globalizations* 11, no. 2: 273–87.

————. 2019. "Signaling Reforms through Election Results: How a Moroccan Opposition Party Demobilized Protests." *British Journal of Middle Eastern Studies* (Aug.): 1–19.

————. 2020. "Demobilising the February 20 Movement in Morocco: Regime Strategies during the Arab Spring." *Journal of North African Studies* 25, no. 4: 616–40.

Baldwin, Kate. 2005. "Who Gets the Jobs? Dynamics of Opposition and Redistribution in Mali." Unpublished paper, Department of Political Science, Columbia Univ.

Bank, André, Thomas Richter, and Anna Sunik. 2015. "Long-Term Monarchical Survival in the Middle East: A Configurational Comparison, 1945–2012." *Democratization* 22, no. 1: 179–200.

Barany, Zoltan. 2013. "Unrest and State Response in Arab Monarchies." *Mediterranean Quarterly* 24, no. 2: 5–38.

Beaumont, Peter. 2016. "Moroccan Police among 11 Investigated over Man Crushed in Rubbish Truck." *Guardian*, Nov. 1, 2016. https://www.the guardian.com/world/2016/nov/01/morocco-police-among-11-investigated -man-crushed-in-rubbish-truck.

Beinin, Joel, and Frédéric Vairel, eds. 2013. *Social Movements, Mobilization, and Contestation in the Middle East and North Africa.* Stanford, CA: Stanford Univ. Press.

Benchemsi, Ahmed. 2014. "Morocco's Makhzen and the Haphazard Activists." In *Taking to the Streets: The Transformation of Arab Activism*, edited by Lina Khatib and Ellen Lust, 199–235. Baltimore: Johns Hopkins Univ. Press.

Benford, Robert D. 1993. "Frame Disputes within the Nuclear Disarmament Movement." *Social Forces* 71, no. 3: 677–701.

Benford, Robert D., and David A. Snow. 2000. "Framing Processes and Social Movements: An Overview and Assessment." *Annual Review of Sociology* 26, no. 1: 611–39.

Benkler, Yochai. 2013. "Practical Anarchism: Peer Mutualism, Market Power, and the Fallible State." *Politics & Society* 41, no. 2: 213–51.

Bennani-Chraïbi, Mounia, Mohamed Jeghllaly, and Sarah-Louise Raillard. 2012. "The Protest Dynamics of Casablanca's February 20th Movement." *Revue Française de Science Politique* 62, no. 5: 867–94.

Bergh, Sylvia I. 2012. "'Inclusive' Neoliberalism, Local Governance Reforms and the Redeployment of State Power: The Case of the National Initiative for

Human Development (INDH) in Morocco." *Mediterranean Politics* 17, no. 3: 410–26.

Blaydes, Lisa. 2010. *Elections and Distributive Politics in Mubarak's Egypt.* Cambridge: Cambridge Univ. Press.

Bouhmouch, Nadir, dir. 2011. *My Makhzen & Me.*

Boukhars, Anouar. 2010. *Politics in Morocco: Executive Monarchy and Enlightened Authoritarianism.* New York: Routledge.

———. 2011. "Political Violence in North Africa: The Perils of Incomplete Liberalization." *Brookings Doha Center Analysis Paper,* no. 3 (Jan.): 1–45.

Boukhars, Anouar, and Shadi Hamid. 2011. "Morocco's Moment of Reform?" Brookings Institution, June 28, 2011. https://www.brookings.edu/opinions/moroccos-moment-of-reform/.

Bradley, John R. 2012. *After the Arab Spring: How Islamists Hijacked the Middle East Revolts.* New York: St. Martin's Press.

Brouksy, Omar. 2011. "Maroc: Des jeunes manifestent pour plus de démocratie." La Presse, June 20, 2011. https://www.lapresse.ca/international/afrique/201106/20/01-4410770-maroc-des-jeunes-manifestent-pour-plus-de-democratie.php.

Brown, Nathan J. 2012. *When Victory Is Not an Option: Islamist Movements in Arab Politics.* Ithaca, NY: Cornell Univ. Press.

Brownlee, Jason. 2007. *Authoritarianism in an Age of Democratization.* Cambridge: Cambridge Univ. Press.

———. 2012. *Democracy Prevention: The Politics of the US-Egyptian Alliance.* Cambridge: Cambridge Univ. Press.

Brownlee, Jason, Tarek E. Masoud, and Andrew Reynolds. 2015. *The Arab Spring: Pathways of Repression and Reform.* Oxford: Oxford Univ. Press.

Brumberg, Daniel. 2002. "Democratization in the Arab World? The Trap of Liberalized Autocracy." *Journal of Democracy* 13, no. 4: 56–68.

———. 2005. "Islam Is Not the Solution (or the Problem)." *Washington Quarterly* 29, no. 1: 97–116.

———. 2013. "Transforming the Arab World's Protection-Racket Politics." *Journal of Democracy* 24, no. 3: 88–103.

Buehler, Matt. 2013a. "Safety-Valve Elections and the Arab Spring: The Weakening (and Resurgence) of Morocco's Islamist Opposition Party." *Terrorism and Political Violence* 25, no. 1: 137–56.

———. 2013b. "The Threat to 'Un-moderate': Moroccan Islamists and the Arab Spring." *Middle East Law and Governance* 5, no. 3: 231–57.

———. 2015. "Labour Demands, Regime Concessions: Moroccan Unions and the Arab Uprising." *British Journal of Middle Eastern Studies* 42, no. 1: 88–103.

———. 2018. *Why Alliances Fail: Islamist and Leftist Coalitions in North Africa.* Syracuse, NY: Syracuse Univ. Press.

Çakmak, Cenap, ed. 2017. *The Arab Spring, Civil Society, and Innovative Activism.* New York: Palgrave Macmillan.

Carey, Sabine C. 2006. "The Dynamic Relationship between Protest and Repression." *Political Research Quarterly* 59, no. 1: 1–11.

Cavatorta, Francesco. 2007. "Neither Participation nor Revolution: The Strategy of the Moroccan Jamiat al-Adl wal-Ihsan." *Mediterranean Politics* 12, no. 3: 381–97.

———. 2009. "'Divided They Stand, Divided They Fail': Opposition Politics in Morocco." *Democratization* 16, no. 1: 137–56.

———. 2016. "Morocco: The Promise of Democracy and the Reality of Authoritarianism." *International Spectator* 51, no. 1: 86–98.

Chikhi, Lamine. 2011. "Algerian President Promises Major Political Reforms." Reuters, Apr. 15, 2011. https://www.reuters.com/article/us-algeria-bouteflika -speech/algerian-president-promises-major-political-reforms-idUSTRE73 E7PF20110415.

Cox, Gary W. 2009. "Authoritarian Elections and Leadership Succession, 1975–2004." Paper presented at the meeting of the American Political Science Association, Toronto.

Cretois, Jules. 2017. "Moroccan Salafists Seek a Voice in the Political Landscape." *Middle East Eye*, Jan. 5, 2017. https://www.middleeasteye.net/features/moroccan -salafists-seek-voice-political-landscape.

Culbertson, Shelly. 2016. *The Fires of Spring: A Post-Arab Spring Journey through the Turbulent New Middle East—Turkey, Iraq, Qatar, Jordan, Egypt, and Tunisia.* New York: St. Martin's Press.

Dalmasso, Emanuela. 2012. "Surfing the Democratic Tsunami in Morocco: Apolitical Society and the Reconfiguration of a Sustainable Authoritarian Regime." *Mediterranean Politics* 17, no. 2: 217–32.

Dalmasso, Emanuela, and Francesco Cavatorta. 2013. "Democracy, Civil Liberties and the Role of Religion after the Arab Awakening: Constitutional Reforms in Tunisia and Morocco." *Mediterranean Politics* 18, no. 2: 225–41.

Daniels, Arlene Kaplan. 1983. "Self-Deception and Self-Discovery in Fieldwork." *Qualitative Sociology* 6, no. 3: 195–214.

Davenport, Christian. 2015. *How Social Movements Die*. Cambridge: Cambridge Univ. Press.

Dawisha, Adeed. 2013. *The Second Arab Awakening: Revolution, Democracy, and the Islamist Challenge from Tunis to Damascus*. New York: W. W. Norton.

De Mesquita, Ethan Bueno. 2010. "Regime Change and Revolutionary Entrepreneurs." *American Political Science Review* 104, no. 3: 446–66.

D'emilio, John. 2012. *Sexual Politics, Sexual Communities*. Chicago: Univ. of Chicago Press.

Den Hond, Frank, Frank G. A. De Bakker, and Nikolai Smith. 2015. "Social Movements and Organizational Analysis." In *The Oxford Handbook of Social Movements*, edited by Donatella Della Porta and Mario Dani, 291–305. Oxford: Oxford Univ. Press.

Desrues, Thierry. 2013. "Mobilizations in a Hybrid Regime: The 20th February Movement and the Moroccan Regime." *Current Sociology* 61, no. 4: 409–23.

Diouani, Azz Eddine. 2021. "Exploring the Voices of the Rif Hirak Activism: The Struggle for Democracy in Morocco." *Mediterranean Politics* (Apr.): 1–26.

Dixon, Marc, and Andrew W. Martin. 2012. "We Can't Win This on Our Own: Unions, Firms, and Mobilization of External Allies in Labor Disputes." *American Sociological Review* 77, no. 6: 946–69.

Dolgon, Corey. 2001. *Building Community amid the Ruins: Strategies for Struggle from the Coalition for Justice at Southampton College*. Lanham, MD: Rowman & Littlefield.

Edwards, Bob, and Sam Marullo. 1995. "Organizational Mortality in a Declining Social Movement: The Demise of Peace Movement Organizations in the End of the Cold War Era." *American Sociological Review* (Dec.): 908–27.

Ellens, J. Harold, ed. 2013. *Winning Revolutions: The Psychosocial Dynamics of Revolts for Freedom, Fairness, and Rights: The Psychosocial Dynamics of Revolts for Freedom, Fairness, and Rights*. Santa Barbara, CA: ABC-CLIO.

Ellman, Matthew, and Leonard Wantchekon. 2000. "Electoral Competition under the Threat of Political Unrest." *Quarterly Journal of Economics* 115, no. 2: 499–531.

Emiljanowicz, Paul. 2017. "Facebook, Mamfakinch, and the February 20 Movement in Morocco." Participedia, July 24, 2017. http://participedia.net/en /cases/facebook-mamfakinch-and-february-20-movement-morocco.

Engelcke, Dörthe. 2016. "Morocco's Changing Civil Society." Carnegie Endowment for International Peace, Jan. 7, 2016. http://carnegieendowment.org/sada/?fa=62417.

Ennaji, Moha. 2016. "About North African Women's Rights after the Arab Spring." In *Women's Movements in Post-"Arab Spring" North Africa*, edited by Fatima Sidiqi, 97–107. New York: Palgrave Macmillan.

EUSpring. 2014. "Timeline Morocco." Univ. of Warwick. Accessed Mar. 16, 2018. http://www2.warwick.ac.uk/fac/soc/pais/research/researchcentres/irs/euspring/advisoryboard/morocco_timeline_2010-2014.pdf.

Fakim, Nora, and Nouri Verghese. 2014. "Where Are Morocco's Revolutionary Activists?" Al-Jazeera, Aug. 19, 2014. https://www.aljazeera.com/news/middleeast/2014/07/where-are-morocco-revolutionary-activists-201472113126388 44.html.

Fakir, Intissar. 2017. "Morocco's Islamist Party: Redefining Politics under Pressure." Carnegie Endowment for International Peace, Dec. 28, 2017. https://carnegieendowment.org/2017/12/28/morocco-s-islamist-party-redefining-politics-under-pressure-pub-75121.

Fearon, James D. 2011 "Self-Enforcing Democracy." *Quarterly Journal of Economics* 126, no. 4: 1661–1708.

Feather, Ginger. 2014. "Competing Frameworks: Feminists Differ over Best Path to Moroccan Women's Rights." *Journal of Women and Human Rights in the Middle East*, no. 2: 19–41.

Francisco, Ronald A. 1995. "The Relationship between Coercion and Protest: An Empirical Evaluation in Three Coercive States." *Journal of Conflict Resolution* 39, no. 2: 263–82.

———. 2004. "After the Massacre: Mobilization in the Wake of Harsh Repression." *Mobilization: An International Quarterly* 9, no. 2: 107–26.

Freeman, Jo. 1972. "The Tyranny of Structurelessness." *Berkeley Journal of Sociology* 17:151–64.

Gamson, William A. 1975. *The Strategy of Social Protest*. Belmont, CA: Dorsey Press.

Gasim, Gamal. 2014. "Explaining Political Activism in Yemen." In *Taking to the Streets: The Transformation of Arab Activism*, edited by Lina Khatib and Ellen Lust, 109–35. Baltimore: Johns Hopkins Univ. Press.

Gatti, Roberta, Diego F. Angel-Urdinola, Joana Silva, and Andras Bodor. 2014. *Striving for Better Jobs: The Challenge of Informality in the Middle East and North Africa*. Washington, DC: World Bank Group.

Gelvin, James L. 2015. *The Arab Uprisings: What Everyone Needs to Know.* New York: Oxford Univ. Press.

Ghimire, Kléber Bertrand. 2011. *Organization Theory and Transnational Social Movements: Organizational Life and Internal Dynamics of Power Exercise within the Alternative Globalization Movement.* Lanham, MD: Lexington Books.

Gupta, Dipak K., Harinder Singh, and Tom Sprague. 1993. "Government Coercion of Dissidents: Deterrence or Provocation?" *Journal of Conflict Resolution* 37, no. 2: 301–39.

Gurney, Joan Neff, and Kathleen J. Tierney. 1982. "Relative Deprivation and Social Movements: A Critical Look at Twenty Years of Theory and Research." *Sociological Quarterly* 23, no. 1: 33–47.

Gurr, Ted Robert. 2015. *Why Men Rebel.* London: Routledge.

Haas, Mark L., and David W. Lesch. 2013. *The Arab Spring: Change and Resistance in the Middle East.* Boulder, CO: Westview Press.

Haines, Herbert H. 1996. *Against Capital Punishment: The Anti-Death Penalty Movement in America, 1972–1994.* Oxford: Oxford Univ. Press.

Hamblin, Amy. 2015. "The Struggle for Political Legitimacy." In *Arab Spring: Negotiating in the Shadow of the Intifadat,* edited by I. William Zartman. Athens: Univ. of Georgia Press.

Hansen, K. V., and A. I. Garey. 1998. *Families in the US: Kinship and Domestic Politics.* Philadelphia: Temple Univ. Press.

Harris, Kevan. 2012. "The Brokered Exuberance of the Middle Class: An Ethnographic Analysis of Iran's 2009 Green Movement." *Mobilization: An International Quarterly* 17, no. 4: 435–55.

Heaney, Michael, and Fabio Rojas. 2011. "The Partisan Dynamics of Contention: Demobilization of the Antiwar Movement in the United States, 2007–2009." *Mobilization: An International Quarterly* 16, no. 1: 45–64.

Hespress. 2017. "من الحركة من أجل الأمة إلى حزب الأمة." Accessed Sept. 5, 2019. http://www.hespress.com/politique/4874.html.

Heydemann, Steven, and Reinoud Leenders. 2011. "Authoritarian Learning and Authoritarian Resilience: Regime Responses to the 'Arab Awakening.'" *Globalizations* 8, no. 5: 647–53.

Hissouf, Abdellatif. 2016. "The Moroccan Monarchy and the Islam-Oriented PJD: Pragmatic Cohabitation and the Need for Islamic Political Secularism." *Journal of Foreign Policy & Peace* 5, no. 1: 43–56.

Hoffmann, Anja, and Christoph König. 2013. "Scratching the Democratic Façade: Framing Strategies of the 20 February Movement." *Mediterranean Politics* 18, no. 1: 1–22.

Holzhacker, Ronald. "'Gay Rights Are Human Rights': The Framing of New Interpretations of International Human Rights Norms." In *The Uses and Misuses of Human Rights*, 29–64. New York: Palgrave Macmillan.

Houry, Nadim. 2010. "Syria's Decade of Repression." *Guardian*, July 16, 2010. http://www.theguardian.com/commentisfree/2010/jul/16/syria-decade -repression-bashar-al-assad.

Huang, Haifeng. 2015. "Propaganda as Signaling." *Comparative Politics* 47, no. 4: 419–44.

Human Rights Watch. 2011. "Morocco: Thousands March for Reform." Feb. 20, 2011. https://www.hrw.org/news/2011/02/20/morocco-thousands-march -reform.

———. 2018. "Morocco: Journalist Convicted on Dubious Charge." July 18, 2018. https://www.hrw.org/news/2018/07/18/morocco-journalist-convicted -dubious-charge.

Humphreys, Macartan, and Jeremy M. Weinstein. 2007. "Demobilization and Reintegration." *Journal of Conflict Resolution* 51, no. 4: 531–67.

Idrissi, Sarra. 2012. "20 February Movement: Reflections of Young Activists." Inclusive Democracy, Mar. 30, 2012. https://www.opendemocracy.net/5050 /sarra-el-idrissi/february-20-movement-reflections-of-young-activist.

Ilahiane, Hsain. 2019. "Why Do Protests Keep Happening in North Africa? It's al-Hogra." Juan Cole, Jan. 22, 2019. https://www.juancole.com/2019/01 /protests-happening-africa.html.

Israeli, Raphael. 2017. *From Arab Spring to Islamic Winter*. New York: Routledge.

Jebnoun, Noureddine. 2020. "Public Space Security and Contentious Politics of Morocco's Rif Protests." *Middle Eastern Studies* 56, no. 1: 48–63.

Johnston, Hank, and John A. Noakes, eds. 2005. *Frames of Protest: Social Movements and the Framing Perspective*. Lanham, MD: Rowman & Littlefield.

Jones, Andrew W., Richard N. Hutchinson, Nella Van Dyke, Leslie Gates, and Michele Companion. 2001. "Coalition Form and Mobilization Effectiveness in Local Social Movements." *Sociological Spectrum* 21, no. 2: 207–31.

Kadivar, Mohammad Ali. 2017. "Preelection Mobilization and Electoral Outcome in Authoritarian Regimes." *Mobilization* 22, no. 3: 293–310.

Kahl, Said al-. 2011. "Background of the Withdrawal of the Justice and Charity Group from the February 20 Movement." *Hespress*, Dec. 28, 2011. https://www.hespress.com/writers/44159.html.

Karam, Souhail. 2011a. "Moroccan Protesters Demand Limit on Royal Powers." Reuters, Feb. 20, 2011. https://www.reuters.com/article/us-morocco-protests-idUSTRE71I3VY20110220.

———. 2011b. "Moroccans Protest Polls, Violence in the Capital." Reuters, Oct. 23, 2011. https://www.reuters.com/article/us-morocco-protests/moroccans-protest-polls-violence-in-the-capital-idUSTRE79M3ZU20111023.

———. 2011c. "Thousands of Moroccans Protest, Unmoved by Reforms." Reuters, July 3, 2011. https://www.reuters.com/article/us-morocco-reform-protests/thousands-of-moroccans-protest-unmoved-by-reforms-idUSTRE7622KP20110703.

———. 2020. "Morocco Rolls Back Democracy under Cover of Covid-19." Bloomberg, July 23, 2020. https://www.bloomberg.com/news/articles/2020-07-24/covid-crackdown-snuffs-out-flickering-embers-of-the-arab-spring.

Köhler, Kevin. 2010. "'All the Kings Men': The Emergence of the Authenticity and Modernity Party (PAM) in Morocco." *IPRIS Magreb Review* (Oct.): 1–15.

Koopmans, Ruud. 1993. "The Dynamics of Protest Waves: West Germany, 1965 to 1989." *American Sociological Review* (Oct.): 637–58.

———. 1997. "Dynamics of Repression and Mobilization: The German Extreme Right in the 1990s." *Mobilization: An International Quarterly* 2, no. 2: 149–64.

———. 2005. "Repression and the Public Sphere: Discursive Opportunities for Repression against the Extreme Right in Germany in the 1990s." In *Repression and Mobilization* edited by Christian Davenport, Hank Johnson, and Carol Mueller, 58–81. Minneapolis: Univ. of Minnesota Press.

Kuran, Timur. 1989. "Sparks and Prairie Fires: A Theory of Unanticipated Political Revolution." *Public Choice* 61, no. 1: 41–74.

———. 1991. "Now Out of Never: The Element of Surprise in the East European Revolution of 1989." *World Politics: A Quarterly Journal of International Relations* (June): 7–48.

Kvale, Steinar. 2008. *Doing Interviews*. Los Angeles: Sage.

Laachir, Karima. 2012. "Managed Reforms and Deferred Democratic Rule in Morocco and Algeria." In *Democracy and Reform in the Middle East and Asia: Social Protest and Authoritarian Rule after the Arab Spring*, edited by Amin Saikal and Amitav Acharya. London: Bloomsbury.

Lavine, Marc, J. Adam Cobb, and Christopher J. Roussin. 2017. "When Saying Less Is Something New: Social Movements and Frame-Contraction Processes." *Mobilization* 22, no. 3: 275–92.

Lawrence, Adria K. 2017. "Repression and Activism among the Arab Spring's First Movers: Evidence from Morocco's February 20th Movement." *British Journal of Political Science* 47, no. 3: 699–718.

Lazare, Sarah. 2011. "Democracy Protesters Face Violence in Morocco." Al-Jazeera, June 21, 2011. http://www.aljazeera.com/indepth/features/2011/06/201162181335141963.html.

Lichbach, Mark Irving. 1987. "Deterrence or Escalation? The Puzzle of Aggregate Studies of Repression and Dissent." *Journal of Conflict Resolution* 31, no. 2: 266–97.

———. 1998. *The Rebel's Dilemma*. Ann Arbor: Univ. of Michigan Press.

Linden, Annette, and Bert Klandermans. 2006. "Stigmatization and Repression of Extreme-Right Activism in the Netherlands." *Mobilization: An International Quarterly* 11, no. 2: 213–28.

Little, Andrew T. 2012. "Elections, Fraud, and Election Monitoring in the Shadow of Revolution." *Quarterly Journal of Political Science* 7, no. 3: 249–83.

———. 2013. *An Informational Theory of Elections*. New York: New York Univ.

———. 2015. "Fraud and Monitoring in Non-competitive Elections." *Political Science Research and Methods* 3, no. 1: 21–41.

Little, Andrew T., Joshua A. Tucker, and Tom LaGatta. 2015. "Elections, Protest, and Alternation of Power." *Journal of Politics* 77, no. 4: 1142–56.

Lohmann, Susanne. 1994. "The Dynamics of Informational Cascades: The Monday Demonstrations in Leipzig, East Germany, 1989–91." *World Politics* 47, no. 1: 42–101.

Londregan, John, and Andrea Vindigni. 2008. "Authoritarian Plebiscites." Unpublished manuscript, Princeton Univ.

Lust-Okar, Ellen. 2006. "Elections under Authoritarianism: Preliminary Lessons from Jordan." *Democratization* 13, no. 3: 456–71.

———. 2012. "Change and Continuity in Elections after the Arab Uprisings." *Swiss Political Science Review* 18, no. 1: 110–13.

Lust-Okar, Ellen, and Amaney Ahmad Jamal. 2002. "Rulers and Rules: Reassessing the Influence of Regime Type on Electoral Law Formation." *Comparative Political Studies* 35, no. 3: 337–66.

Lynch, Marc. 2013. *The Arab Uprising: The Unfinished Revolutions of the New Middle East*. New York: Public Affairs.

Maddy-Weitzman, Bruce. 2011. *The Berber Identity Movement and the Challenge to North African States*. Austin: Univ. of Texas Press.

Magaloni, Beatriz. 2006. *Voting for Autocracy: Hegemonic Party Survival and Its Demise in Mexico*. Vol. 296. Cambridge: Cambridge Univ. Press.

Maghraoui, Driss. 2011. "Constitutional Reforms in Morocco: Between Consensus and Subaltern Politics." *Journal of North African Studies* 16, no. 4: 679–99.

Mainwaring, Scott, and Timothy Scully, eds. 1995. *Building Democratic Institutions: Party Systems in Latin America*. Stanford, CA: Stanford Univ. Press.

Marsh, Katherine. 2011. "Syria Protests Continue as Bashar al-Assad Promises Reform." *Observer*, Apr. 16, 2011. http://www.theguardian.com/world/2011/apr/16/bashar-al-assad-syria.

Masbah, Mohammed. 2017. "A New Generation of Protests in Morocco? How Hirak al-Rif Endures." *Arab Reform Initiative Policy Alternatives* (Nov.): 1–10. https://www.arab-reform.net/publication/a-new-generation-of-protests-in-morocco-how-hirak-al-rif-endures/.

Mason, T. David, and Dale A. Krane. 1989. "The Political Economy of Death Squads: Toward a Theory of the Impact of State-Sanctioned Terror." *International Studies Quarterly* 33, no. 2: 175–98.

McAdam, Doug. 1983. "Tactical Innovation and the Pace of Insurgency." *American Sociological Review* 48, no. 6: 735–54.

———. 2010. *Political Process and the Development of Black Insurgency, 1930–1970*. Chicago: Univ. of Chicago Press.

McAdam, Doug, John D. McCarthy, and Mayer N. Zald. 1988. "Social Movements." In *Handbook of Sociology*, edited by N. J. Smelser, 695–737. Newbury Park, CA: Sage.

———, eds. 1996. *Comparative Perspectives on Social Movements: Political Opportunities, Mobilizing Structures, and Cultural Framings*. Cambridge: Cambridge Univ. Press.

McAdam, Doug, Sidney Tarrow, and Charles Tilly. 2003. "Dynamics of Contention." *Social Movement Studies* 2, no. 1: 99–102.

———. 2009. "Comparative Perspectives on Contentious Politics." In *Comparative Politics: Rationality, Culture, and Structure*, edited by Mark Lichbach and Alan Zuckerman, 260–90. Cambridge: Cambridge Univ. Press.

McCammon, Holly J., and Minyoung Moon. 2015. "Social Movement Coalitions." In *The Oxford Handbook of Social Movements*, edited by Donatella Della Porta and Mario Dani. Oxford: Oxford Univ. Press.

Mekouar, Merouan. 2010. "Moroccan Islamists: All the Taste, Half the Calories." Midwest Political Science Association meeting.

———. 2016. *Protest and Mass Mobilization: Authoritarian Collapse and Political Change in North Africa*. Routledge: London.

Mesbah, Mohamed. 2015. "What Remains of the February 20 Movement." Carnegie Endowment for International Peace, Feb. 23, 2015. https://carnegie-mec.org/2015/02/23/ar-pub-59186.

Meyer, David, and Catherine Corrigall-Brown. "Coalitions and Political Context: US Movements against Wars in Iraq." *Mobilization: An International Quarterly* 10, no. 3: 327–44.

Meyer, David S., and Debra C. Minkoff. 2004. "Conceptualizing Political Opportunity." *Social Forces* 82, no. 4: 1457–92.

Mitiche, Ahmed Zakarya. 2017. "Morocco's February 20 Movement: 'Demands Still Alive.'" Al-Jazeera, Feb. 22, 2017. https://www.aljazeera.com/indepth/features/2017/02/morocco-february-20-movement-demands-alive-170222063934604.html.

Molina, Irene Fernandez. 2011. "The Monarchy vs. the 20 February Movement: Who Holds the Reins of Political Change in Morocco?" *Mediterranean Politics* 16, no. 3: 435–41.

Monjib, Maâti. 2011. "The 'Democratization' Process in Morocco: Progress, Obstacles, and the Impact of the Islamist-Secularist Divide." Saban Center for Middle East Policy, Brookings Institution, Aug. 12, 2011. https://www.brookings.edu/research/the-democratization-process-in-morocco-progress-obstacles-and-the-impact-of-the-islamist-secularist-divide/.

———. 2020. "The Moroccan Spring Is Back: The Rif Hirak." In *The Unfinished Arab Spring: Micro-dynamics of Revolts between Change and Continuity*, edited by Fatima El-Issawi and Francesco Cavatorta, 112–35. London: Ginko Library.

Mouline, Nabil. 2015. "Reconsidering the Rif Revolt (1958–59)." Jadaliyya, Jan. 28, 2015. http://www.jadaliyya.com/pages/index/20664/reconsidering-the-rif-revolt-(1958-59).

National Democratic Institute. 2011. "Final Report on the Moroccan Legislative Elections." ndi.org/sites/default/files/Morocco-Final-Election-Report-061812-ENG.pdf.

Naudé, Pierre-François. 2011. "Le bilan des manifestations au Maroc s'élève à cinq morts et 128 blessés." JeuneAfrique, Feb. 21, 2011. http://www.jeuneafrique

.com/182305/politique/le-bilan-des-manifestations-au-maroc-s-l-ve-cinq
-morts-et-128-bless-s/.

Nossiter, Adam. 2019. "In an Epic Standoff, Unarmed Algerians Get the Army to
Blink." *New York Times*, July 29, 2019. https://www.nytimes.com/2019/07/29
/world/africa/algeria-revolution-standoff.html.

Noueihed, Lin, and Alex Warren. 2012. *The Battle for the Arab Spring: Revolution, Counter-revolution and the Making of a New Era*. New Haven, CT: Yale
Univ. Press.

Ohnuki-Tierney, Emiko. 1984. "'Native' Anthropologists." *American Ethnolo-
gist* 11, no. 3: 584–86.

Okamoto, Dina G. 2010. "Organizing across Ethnic Boundaries in the Post–Civil
Rights Era: Asian American Panethnic Coalitions." In *Strategic Alliances:
Coalition Building and Social Movements*, edited by Nella Van Dyke and
Holly McCammon, 143–69. Minneapolis: Univ. of Minnesota Press.

Olcott, Martha Brill, and Marina Ottaway. 1999. "The Challenge of Semiauthoritarianism." Carnegie Paper No. 7. https://carnegieendowment.org
/files/DemChallenged_Intro.pdf.

Ortega, Daniel, and Michael Penfold-Becerra. 2008. "Does Clientelism Work?
Electoral Returns of Excludable and Non-excludable Goods in Chavez's Mis-
iones Programs in Venezuela." Paper presented at the meeting of the American Political Science Association.

Ottaway, Marina. 2011. "The New Moroccan Constitution: Real Change or More
of the Same?" Carnegie Endowment for International Peace, June 20, 2011.
https://carnegieendowment.org/2011/06/20/new-moroccan-constitution
-real-change-or-more-of-same-pub-44731.

Oumlil, Kenza. 2017. "Making Sense of Recent Protests in Morocco." Al-Jazeera,
June 4, 2017. http://www.aljazeera.com/indepth/opinion/2017/06/making
-sense-protests-morocco-170604092533766.html.

Paolini, Isabel. 2017. "A Deeper Look at the Protests in Morocco." POMED, June 1,
2017. https://pomed.org/a-deeper-look-at-the-protests-in-morocco-updated/.

Pellicer, Miquel, and Eva Wegner. 2015. "The Justice and Development Party in
Moroccan Local Politics." *Middle East Journal* 69, no. 1: 32–50.

Pellicer, Miquel, Eva Wegner, and Francesco Cavatorta. 2015. "Is There Strength
in Numbers?" *Middle East Law and Governance* 7, no. 1: 153–68.

Pierskalla, Jan Henryk. 2010. "Protest, Deterrence, and Escalation: The Strategic
Calculus of Government Repression." *Journal of Conflict Resolution* 54, no.
1: 117–45.

Polletta, Francesca, and James M. Jasper. 2001. "Collective Identity and Social Movements." *Annual Review of Sociology* 27, no. 1: 283–305.

Prashad, Vijay. 2012. *Arab Spring, Libyan Winter*. Oakland, CA: AK Press.

Przeworski, Adam. 1991. *Democracy and the Market: Political and Economic Reforms in Eastern Europe and Latin America*. Cambridge: Cambridge Univ. Press.

Rachidi, Ilhem. 2015. "Inside the Movement: What Is Left of Morocco's February 20." *Middle East Eye*, Feb. 26, 2015. https://www.middleeasteye.net/features /inside-movement-what-left-moroccos-february-20.

———. 2017. "The Hirak: A Moroccan People's Movement Demands Change from the Streets." Toward Freedom, Dec. 20, 2017. https://towardfreedom.org /story/archives/africa-archives/hirak-moroccan-peoples-movement-demands -change-streets/.

———. 2019. "Morocco's Crackdown Won't Silence Dissent." *Foreign Policy*, Jan. 16, 2019. https://foreignpolicy.com/2019/01/16/moroccos-crackdown-wont -silence-dissent-maroc-hirak-amdh/.

Radi, Abdelaziz. 2017. "Protest Movements and Social Media: Morocco's February 20 Movement." *Africa Development* 42, no. 2: 31–55.

Rahman, Zahir. 2011. "Morocco's Bottom-Up Movement for Reform." *Foreign Policy* (blog), Dec. 13, 2011. https://foreignpolicy.com/2011/12/13/moroccos -bottom-up-movement-for-reform/.

Rasler, Karen. 1996. "Concessions, Repression, and Political Protest in the Iranian Revolution." *American Sociological Review* (Feb.): 132–52.

Reporters without Borders. 2017. "RSF Responds to Morocco's Culture and Communication Ministry." Aug. 18, 2017. https://rsf.org/en/news/rsf-responds -moroccos-culture-and-communication-ministry.

Roth, Benita. 2010. "'Organizing One's Own' as Good Politics: Second Wave Feminists and the Meaning of Coalition." In *Strategic Alliances: Coalition Building and Social Movements*, edited by Nella Van Dyke and Holly J. McCammon, 99–118. Minneapolis: Univ. of Minnesota Press.

Rozenas, Arturas. 2012. "Elections, Information, and Political Survival in Autocracies." PhD diss., Duke Univ.

Rubin, Herbert J., and Irene S. Rubin. 2011. *Qualitative Interviewing: The Art of Hearing Data*. Thousand Oaks, CA: Sage.

Ryan, Curtis R. 2018. *Jordan and the Arab Uprisings*. New York: Columbia Univ. Press.

Sakthivel, Vish. 2014. *Al-Adl wal-Ihsan: Inside Morocco's Islamist Challenge*. Washington, DC: Washington Institute for Near East Policy.

Shearlaw, Maeve. 2016. "Moroccan Activists Plan Protests to Coincide with UN Climate Summit." *Guardian*, Nov. 5, 2016. https://www.theguardian.com /world/2016/nov/05/moroccan-activists-plan-protests-un-climate-summit -marrakech.

Simpser, Alberto. 2013. *Why Governments and Parties Manipulate Elections: Theory, Practice, and Implications*. Cambridge: Cambridge Univ. Press.

Snow, David A., and Robert D. Benford. 1988. "Ideology, Frame Resonance, and Participant Mobilization." *International Social Movement Research* 1, no. 1: 197–217.

———. 1992. "Master Frames and Cycles of Protest." In *Frontiers in Social Movement Theory*, edited by Aldon Morris and Carol Mueller, 133–55. New Haven, CT: Yale Univ. Press.

Sotiropoulos, George. 2017. "Staging Democracy: The Aganaktismenoi of Greece and the Squares Movement(s)." *Contention* 5, no. 1: 84–107.

Spiegel, Avi Max. 2015. *Young Islam: The New Politics of Religion in Morocco and the Arab World*. Princeton, NJ: Princeton Univ. Press.

Stacher, Joshua. 2012. *Adaptable Autocrats: Regime Power in Egypt and Syria*. Stanford, CA: Stanford Univ. Press.

Staggenborg, Suzanne. 2010. "Conclusion: Research on Social Movement Coalitions." In *Strategic Alliances: Coalition Building and Social Movements*, edited by Nella Van Dyke and Holly McCammon, 316–29. Minneapolis: Univ. of Minnesota Press.

Taber, Nancy. 2010. "Institutional Ethnography, Autoethnography, and Narrative: An Argument for Incorporating Multiple Methodologies." *Qualitative Research* 10, no. 1: 5–25.

Tarrow, Sidney. 1994. "Social Movements in Europe: Movement Society or Europeanization of Conflict?" Unpublished paper.

Touati, Zeineb. 2013. "The Struggle for Women's Rights in Morocco: From Historical Feminism to 20 February 2011 Activism." In *Arab Spring and Arab Women*, edited by Muhamad Olimat, 121–33. New York: Routledge.

Tucker, Joshua A. 2007. "Enough! Electoral Fraud, Collective Action Problems, and Post-communist Colored Revolutions." *Perspectives on Politics* 5, no. 3: 535–51.

Tufekci, Zeynep. 2017. *Twitter and Tear Gas: The Power and Fragility of Networked Protest*. New Haven, CT: Yale Univ. Press.

Van Dyke, Nella. 2003. "Crossing Movement Boundaries: Factors That Facilitate Coalition Protest by American College Students, 1930–1990." *Social Problems* 50, no. 2: 226–50.

Van Dyke, Nella, and Holly J. McCammon. 2010. *Strategic Alliances: Coalition Building and Social Movements.* Minneapolis: Univ. of Minnesota Press.

Wang, Dan J., and Sarah A. Soule. 2016. "Tactical Innovation in Social Movements: The Effects of Peripheral and Multi-issue Protest." *American Sociological Review* 81, no. 3: 517–48.

Wang Xu, Yu Ye, and Chris King-chi Chan. 2019. "Space in a Social Movement: A Case Study of Occupy Central in Hong Kong in 2014." *Space and Culture* 22, no. 4: 434–48.

Ward, Matthew. 2009. "Democracy and Authoritarianism in the Middle East." PhD diss., Univ. of Michigan.

Waterbury, John. 1970. *The Commander of the Faithful: The Moroccan Political Elite, a Study in Segmented Politics.* London: Weidenfeld & Nicolson.

Wedeen, Lisa. 2015. *Ambiguities of Domination: Politics, Rhetoric, and Symbols in Contemporary Syria.* Chicago: Univ. of Chicago Press.

Wegner, Eva. 2011. *Islamist Opposition in Authoritarian Regimes: The Party of Justice and Development in Morocco.* Syracuse, NY: Syracuse Univ. Press.

Wegner, Eva, and Miquel Pellicer. 2011. "Left–Islamist Opposition Cooperation in Morocco." *British Journal of Middle Eastern Studies* 38, no. 3: 303–22.

Weingast, B. R. 1997. "The Political Foundations of Democracy and the Rule of Law." *American Political Science Review* 19, no. 2: 245–63.

Whalen, Jack, and Richard Flacks. 1989. *Beyond the Barricades: The Sixties Generation Grows Up.* Philadelphia: Temple Univ. Press.

Willis, Michael. 2014. *Politics and Power in the Maghreb: Algeria, Tunisia and Morocco from Independence to the Arab Spring.* Oxford: Oxford Univ. Press.

Wolf, Anne. 2019. "Morocco's Hirak Movement and Legacies of Contention in the Rif." *Journal of North African Studies* 24, no. 1: 1–6.

Yitzhak, Ronen. 2017. "From Cooperation to Normalization? Jordan–Israel Relations since 1967." *British Journal of Middle Eastern Studies* 44, no. 4: 559–75.

Yom, Sean L., and F. Gregory Gause III. 2012. "Resilient Royals: How Arab Monarchies Hang On." *Journal of Democracy* 23, no. 4: 74–88.

YouTube. 2017. "Morocco Campaign #feb20 #morocco." Accessed Sept. 4, 2019. https://www.youtube.com/watch?v=S0f6FSB7gxQ.

Zald, Mayer N., and Roberta Ash. 1966. "Social Movement Organizations: Growth, Decay and Change." *Social Forces* 44, no. 3: 327–41.

Zartman, I. William. 1988. "Opposition as Support of the State." In *Beyond Coercion: The Durability of the Arab State,* edited by Adeed Dawisha and I. William Zartman, 61–87. New York: Routledge.

Index

Italic page numbers denote illustrations.

183

SAMMY ZEYAD BADRAN is an assistant professor of political science at the American University of Sharjah, UAE. He received his PhD from the University of Kansas, Department of Political Science, in 2018. His research focuses on the contentious politics and social movements within the Middle East and North Africa. Sammy spent 2016 and 2017 conducting field research in Morocco funded through a Fulbright Research Fellowship where he conducted more than forty-five semistructured interviews with leftist, Islamist, and independent members of civil society organizations and political parties that participated in the February 20 Movement.